# Evidence-based Teaching

A Critical Overview for
Enquiring Teachers

# Evidence-based Teaching

## A Critical Overview for Enquiring Teachers

**Carey Philpott and Val Poultney**

First published in 2018 by Critical Publishing Ltd

British Library Cataloguing in Publication Data

A CIP record for this book is available from the British Library

ISBN: 9781911106722

This book is also available in the following e-book formats:

MOBI ISBN: 9781911106739
EPUB ISBN: 9781911106746
Adobe e-book ISBN: 9781911106753

Cover design by Out of House Limited
Text design by Out of House Limited
Project Management by Out of House Publishing Solutions
Printed and bound in Great Britain by Bell & Bain, Glasgow

Critical Publishing
3 Connaught Road
St Albans
AL3 5RX

 **www.criticalpublishing.com**

For orders and details of our bulk discounts please go to our website or contact our distributor NBN International by telephoning 01752 202301 or emailing orders@nbninternational.com.

# Acknowledgements

I would like to thank Julia Morris of Critical Publishing for giving me the opportunity to complete this book and to Carey Philpott's family for allowing his work to be used to guide the structure of the forthcoming series.

I would also like to thank the teachers and colleagues who have contributed to the case studies that appear in most of the chapters and to Dr Brian Hall for all his stalwart work in proofreading the text.

Finally, thanks again to Julia for all her support as the book was in preparation and to Ian Menter for his supportive comments in reviewing the early draft and drawing my attention to recent literature on randomised controlled trials.

Val Poultney

# Dedication

This book is dedicated to the memory of Professor Carey Philpott who died before he was able to complete this book. He had already written the book proposal and sketched out a few of the chapters so it was an honour and a privilege to be asked by Critical Publishing to complete the book he started. I do hope I have done justice to Carey's vision for this core book in the series *Evidence-based Teaching for Enquiring Teachers* for which he was also series editor. I was also honoured to be asked to take on this role so that we could continue working on this important area of education in his name.

Val Poultney

# Contents

# Meet the series editor and authors

## Val Poultney

is the series editor for *Evidence-based Teaching for Enquiring Teachers* and co-author of this core title in the series. She is a senior lecturer at the University of Derby, teaching on initial teacher education and postgraduate programmes. Her research interests include school leadership and school governance with a particular focus on how to develop leadership to support teachers as researchers.

## Carey Philpott

was Professor of Teacher Education at Leeds Beckett University. Before this he worked at Oxford Brookes University, the University of Cumbria and the University of Strathclyde. Before working in Teacher Education, Carey was an English and Drama teacher in secondary schools in Glasgow and London and a mentor for student teachers on PGCE courses. His research interests included teachers' collaborative professional development, teachers as researchers, evidence-based teaching, and the relationship between teachers' learning and learning in the health professions.

# Chapter 1
# **Mapping the area**

## 1.1  Chapter overview

This chapter will outline:

1.2   an introduction to evidence-based teaching;

1.3   key ideas associated with the drive towards evidence-based teaching;

1.4   the recent history of efforts to establish evidence-based teaching;

1.5   the main lines of argument from both proponents and opponents of
      evidence-based teaching;

1.6   a research map, detailing the evolution of evidence-based teaching and
      current debates.

## 1.2  Introduction

The devolution of schools in England from local authority control has resulted
in great changes to the education landscape and particularly so within the last
decade. Since David Hargreaves's (1996) lecture identifying the lack of impact
of academic educational research on practice, efforts have been made to bring
theory and practice closer together and to demonstrate a positive impact on
the quality of education received by learners. The final report of the BERA-RSA
inquiry into the role of research in teacher education (2014) made clear that
research and teacher inquiry were of paramount importance in developing
self-improving schools. The report advocated a closer working partnership between teacher researchers and the wider academic research community. This
idea is also a notion that is gaining in popularity with providers of professional
development programmes through Teaching School Alliances, Multi-academy
Trusts, Research Schools (https://researchschool.org.uk/), Teaching Schools
(www.gov.uk/guidance/teaching-schools-a-guide-for-potential-applicants;
www.tscouncil.org.uk/) and charities such as the Educational Endowment
Foundation (EEF) (https://educationendowmentfoundation.org.uk).

The Carter Review of Initial Teaching Training (DfE, 2015) made clear that
trainee teachers should have access to, and be able to utilise, research evidence as part of their planning and teaching strategies, which is also noted in
the education White Paper *Educational Excellence Everywhere* (DfE, 2016a). Yet
trainees are not required to demonstrate their research competency as part of

the Teaching Standards, save for engaging in *'appropriate self-reflection, reflection and professional development activity'* (Teachers' Standards, DfE, 2011, p 7), and the opportunities available to them in school to engage with research are sporadic. Hammersley-Fletcher et al (2015) in their interim report about how Teaching School Alliances develop capability and capacity for evidence-based teaching identify a range of limitations that may prevent schools making the transition from research-interested to research-engaged.

Since the work of Goldacre (2013) there has been some resurgence of links with medical models of research: Randomised Controlled Trials (RCTs), Rounds and Clinical models, all of which draw upon an evidence-based approach. This is further highlighted in the British Educational Research Association (BERA) commissioning research into what teacher education can learn from medical education (Baumfield and Mattick, 2017).

## 1.3  Key ideas associated with the drive towards evidence-based teaching

There are a number of key ideas which are associated with evidence-based teaching (EBT) approaches, some of which might be familiar to you as a teacher and others less so. You might think that some of them only belong to the world of academia, such as systematic literature reviews. In later chapters we explore such issues in more depth and offer links not only to school practice, but in ways that may challenge your own thinking about how you use evidence-based approaches in your own work. Figure 1a below presents the interrelationships between different ideas in evidence-based teaching.

### Systematic literature reviews

Most research draws on a range of theoretical literature and a systematic review is conducted to find all existing research on a given topic. That body of literature is then reviewed and evaluated against a range of specific criteria which have been drawn up to test the quality of the research. This reduces large numbers of sources (papers, books, reports) to a few quality publications. The findings of those sources are then synthesised to determine what evidence there is for the value of carrying out particular educational practices. In reality, few practitioners have the time or the resources to carry out these types of literature searches but summaries of such studies are readily accessible to practitioners through, for example, the Educational Endowment Foundation (EEF) Teaching and Learning Toolkit (https://educationendowment foundation.org.uk/evidence/teaching-learning-toolkit). Chapter 2 takes a closer look at systematic literature reviews.

## Figure 1a: Key ideas associated with the drive towards evidence-based teaching

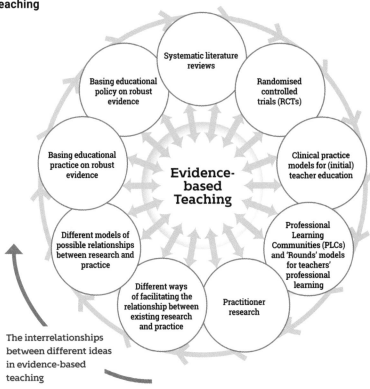

The interrelationships between different ideas in evidence-based teaching

## Randomised controlled trials (RCTs)

RCTs are the most robust research model for finding out what works in education. In RCTs populations of students are assigned randomly to two different groups. One group is taught using the method whose effectiveness is being researched. The other group is either taught as they would normally be (if the normal method does not use the method being tested) or using a different placebo method. Differences in outcome (if there are any) can then be attributed to the effectiveness of the method being researched. Most existing educational research does not involve the use of RCTs, as, for reasons that will be outlined later in the chapter and explored later in this book, many researchers do not consider such trials appropriate for researching educational issues. Typically, RCTs are judged in systematic literature reviews (see above) to be the highest quality research.

### Clinical practice models for (initial) teacher education

These are notionally based on the way in which medical students learn during clinical practice, where consideration of specific real-life cases is the starting point. Student teachers' learning should reflect this practice model with real cases of pupils' learning as the initial stimulus. Using this model to establish a starting point for learning would help us to decide what to do to move the situation forward. This is an evidence-based process because it needs to use:

- evidence of the pupils' current learning and needs;
- evidence (ie from research) of what will help move the situation forward;
- evaluation of the evidence of the outcome of actions taken.

Many advocates of the model also emphasise the use of evidence to improve the model itself.

### Professional learning communities and 'Rounds' models for teachers' professional learning

Professional learning communities (PLCs) are where groups of teachers come together to critically evaluate pupils' learning using their attainment data and classroom observations, where they maintain a focus on pupil learning. They may do this through a process such as lesson study (Dudley, 2014). They use this data as evidence of what is happening in classrooms to develop more effective teaching and learning practice. Rounds models are similar to PLCs but make an explicit link between what teachers do in schools and the medical rounds carried out by doctors. In these Rounds observable evidence of the current situation is generated in order to develop collective professional practice.

### Practitioner research

Practitioner research is an idea and a practice that exists independently of the current drive for evidence-based teaching. However, it is associated with it in several ways, for example through:

- a concern that there is a gap between the educational research community and the practitioner community (ie teachers);
- a belief that medicine has a more effective research/practice relationship;
- ideas like translational research (see below).

### Different ways of facilitating the relationship between existing research and practice

One concern driving evidence-based teaching is the belief that much teaching practice is not based on existing research evidence. This concern is associated with different ideas about facilitating a connection between research evidence and practice. Among these are the following.

- The 'funnel' model, where teachers have access to a wide variety of research findings (via the web, publications, university papers), yet need to be able to reduce or 'funnel' this information with a view to using it in their own teacher inquiries.

- Knowledge mobilisation, which focuses on the factors that lead to existing (generalised) research knowledge being used in specific locations. Concern with knowledge mobilisation recognises that research knowledge cannot necessarily be used 'off the peg' but has to be adapted or rethought to be relevant to particular contexts. It also needs to be actively 'picked up' by practitioners. So it is more than just a question of dissemination or access.

- Translational research, which focuses on the additional (practitioner) research work that needs to be done to explore how to make generalised research findings effective in diverse specific situations.

## Different models of possible relationships between research and practice

If we want teaching to be 'evidence-based', questions about the types of relationships that might exist between research and practice arise. What do we expect that relationship to be? Two possible relationships that recur in academic debate around evidence-based teaching are:

1. The 'engineering' model, where particular research outcomes are thought to have an immediate and direct influence on changing practice.

2. The 'enlightenment' model, where teachers evaluate research outcomes, take a decision either to reject or accept them, followed by a period of implementation to effect the desired change.

## Basing educational *practice* on robust evidence/basing educational *policy* on robust evidence

It is possible to detect a difference in emphasis from different advocates of better use of evidence in education. Some emphasise the necessity of this in the practice of individual teachers, whereas others emphasise the need for practices imposed by government policy to be underpinned by robust evidence. This can be a significant difference. Some argue that insisting that robust evidence underpins the practice of individual teachers can become, in reality, a way of governments extending intrusive centralised control into individual classrooms, leaving no room for practitioners' expert judgement in local circumstances. On the other hand, it is argued that practitioners should be given latitude to make choices about what they do in local circumstances but where practice is mandatorily imposed by government, this is where the robust evidence-base is most needed. So it is a question of where the eye of evidence-based scrutiny is mostly directed: on teachers or on governments. In part, this debate turns on what we mean by evidence in evidence-based practice. This is discussed in the next subsection.

## The interrelationships between different ideas in evidence-based teaching

A number of relationships can exist between each of the ideas outlined in section 1.3. We will not try to cover all of them here, just a few so that you can get a general idea.

For example, what is the relationship between systematic literature reviews and practitioner research? As indicated earlier, systematic literature reviews tend to privilege RCTs as the highest quality form of research. Does this mean that the findings of systematic literature reviews outweigh evidence from practitioner research? If so, does this mean that the dominant model of evidence-based teaching will become one in which systematic literature reviews based on RCTs will 'over-rule' practitioner research in deciding what happens in classrooms? In addition, given that systematic literature reviews and RCTs are resource heavy, does this mean that only large-scale centrally funded evidence will count to determine practice? In turn, does this mean that the dominant way of facilitating the relationship between research and practice will become the 'funnel' model and that the dominant relationship between research and practice will be the engineering model? Will PLCs restrict their work to finding the most efficient ways of implementing centrally dictated practice or will they have a role in developing new practices? And will clinical practice models only use systematic literature reviews as their source of evidence for what to do next?

Another way of thinking about these questions is to recognise that nearly all teaching currently *is* evidence-based. The debate is less about whether teaching should be based on evidence and more about which evidence it should be based on. Should this be, for example, personal experience or a national research project? Or could it be around pupil feedback or systematic literature review? The question of how different *types* of evidence should relate to one another in evidence-based teaching is a central question that is explored later in this chapter (and in the rest of this book!).

## 1.4  The recent history of efforts to establish evidence-based teaching

The following timeline summarises the recent history of evidence-based teaching. The work builds on the legacy of Stenhouse's work (1975) – the teacher as researcher whom he envisaged would research their own practice not only to inform it but to also improve it. This he believed would liberate teachers and enable them to work alongside academic researchers, an emancipatory approach through acquiring knowledge which would in turn help them become 'extended professionals' (Hoyle, 1974).

### Timeline of key dates

### 1996

The Teacher Training Agency Annual Lecture: 'Teaching as Research Based Profession: Possibilities and Prospects' given by David Hargreaves (University of Cambridge). The lecture criticises education research for having an insufficient impact on educational practice and begins the recent period of controversy and debate.

### 1998

Ofsted publishes *Educational Research: A Critique*, authored by James Tooley (University of Newcastle) and Doug Darby (University of Manchester). The report was prompted by Hargreaves' TTA speech. It argued that much education research was partisan, had methodological problems, lacked evidence or coherent argument, was of questionable use to practitioners and was not replicable or cumulative.

### 1998

Department for Education and Employment (DfEE) publishes *Excellence in Research on Schools*, authored by Jim Hillage, Richard Pearson, Alan Anderson and Penny Tamkin (University of Sussex). It concluded that education research tended to:

* be small scale and failed to generate findings that are reliable and generalisable;

* be insufficiently based on existing knowledge and therefore capable of advancing understanding;

* be presented in a form or medium which is largely inaccessible to a non-academic audience;

* lack interpretation for a policy-making or practitioner audience.

**2000**

David Blunkett (Secretary of State for Education) gives a speech to the Economic and Social Research Council (ESRC) titled 'Influence or Irrelevance: Can Social Science Improve Government?', which calls for *'studies which combine large scale, quantitative information on effect sizes which will allow us to generalise'*.

**2000**

Department for Education and Schools (DfES) funds a programme of systematic literature reviews supported by the Evidence for Policy and Practice Information and Co-ordinating (EPPI) Centre at the University of London, Institute of Education. Initially for five years. The results are made available in an online database.

**2000**

Campbell Collaboration established. An online collection of systematic literature reviews for social policy, including education. Inspired by the Cochrane Collaboration on medicine.

**2003**

Centre for the Use of Research and Evidence in Education (CUREE) founded as a private company.

**2007**

EPPI-Centre database of education research is no longer updated.

**2011**

The Department for Education (DfE) appoints the Sutton Trust charity as lead partner in the Education Endowment Foundation (EEF). The EEF's role is to *'develop initiatives to raise the attainment of the poorest pupils in the most challenging schools'*. It hosts the online Teaching and Learning Toolkit of strategies to improve learning, based on reviewing available evidence.

**2013**

The Sutton Trust and EEF jointly designated by the government as the 'What Works' Centre for improving education outcomes for school-aged children. It joins other 'What Works' Centres such as the National Institute for Health and Clinical Excellence (NICE)

**2013**

Ben Goldacre (doctor, author, broadcaster and Research Fellow at the London School of Hygiene and Tropical Medicine) writes *Building Evidence into Education* which is hosted by the DfE website. Goldacre argues for greater use of RCTs in education research.

**2014**

National Foundation for Educational Research (NFER) publishes *Using Evidence in the Classroom: What Works and Why*. The report focuses on how to facilitate knowledge mobilisation. It recommends:

* developing infrastructure, including an institute for excellence similar to healthcare;

* fostering a change in teachers' attitudes to research;

* the need for research bodies to transform evidence for practice, not just synthesise or summarise it, and the need for social interaction in this process;

* more research for better understanding of what works to facilitate knowledge mobilisation.

**2014**

The British Educational Research Association (BERA) and Royal Society for the Encouragement of Arts, Manufactures and Commerce (RSA) publish *Research and the Teaching Profession*. It recommends that:

* teachers need to engage with research;

* teachers need to be equipped to engage in enquiry-based practice;

* a research-rich culture needs to be established at all levels of the education system;

* time and resources need to be made available for research engagement.

**2015**

The charity Education Futures Collaboration hosts the online site MESH Guides as a community to produce and disseminate research summaries for evidence-informed practice.

**2015**

The Carter Review of Initial Teacher Training (published by the Department for

Education [DfE]) calls for evidence-based teaching to be part of the framework for ITT content and for a central portal for evidence-based practice.

## 2015

National College for Teaching and Leadership (NCTL) publishes *Teaching Schools Evaluation*. It concludes (inter alia) that:

* some teaching school alliances are yet to develop their research strand;

* less than half reported substantial changes in the use of research evidence to inform practice;

* securing time and active involvement from classroom teachers remains a major challenge;

* achieving a school-wide and alliance-wide understanding of research in a school context is still to be developed in the majority of case study alliances.

## 2016

DfE publishes the White Paper *Educational Excellence Everywhere*. This sets out the intention to foster an evidence-informed teaching profession by increasing teachers' access to and use of high quality evidence, establishing a new British education journal and expanding the EEF.

## 2017

The British Educational Research Association (BERA) commission a report by Vivienne Baumfield and Karen Mattick (University of Exeter) entitled *Cost, Value and Quality in Professional Learning: Promoting Economic Literacy in Medical and Teacher Education*. This reviewed ways in which education could be supported through various partnerships. The work is still on-going at the time of writing. It recommends that:

* it is possible to bring together medical and teacher educators;

* BERA should facilitate further inter-disciplinary dialogue;

* key personnel from other professions should be consulted to address key educational problems in addition to medical and teacher educators;

* there should be future development of a toolkit for decision-making in professional education.

Chief Executive Professor Dame Alison Peacock opens the Chartered College of Teaching, which is established as the new professional body for education.

## What can we learn from the recent history of evidence-based teaching?

The first thing that might be noteworthy is how long the 'recent' drive for evidence-based teaching has been going on. Newer entrants to the teaching profession might be forgiven for thinking that this drive for evidence-based teaching was a relatively new initiative that perhaps dates back to the early 2010s. However, this is an idea that (in its recent manifestation) has been strongly proposed for 20 years (starting when some of the most recently qualified teachers were still in the early years of primary schooling).

Earlier proponents making the case for evidence-based teaching sound unarguable. For example, in the USA, Slavin (2002, p 17) argued that if education adopted evidence-based practice it *'would experience the step-by-step, irreversible progress characteristic of medicine and agriculture'*. From the UK, Gorard and Torgerson (2006) argued that the rationale for RCTs should be *'patronising to discuss (for even many primary school children know… about a fair test from their science learning)'*. Slavin (2002, p 15) opined that *'Education is on the brink of a scientific revolution that has the potential to profoundly transform policy, practice and research'*.

However, 17 years after the obvious benefits of evidence-based teaching were first outlined by Hargreaves, Goldacre (2013, p 7) felt it necessary to write that:

> **…there is a huge prize waiting to be claimed by teachers. By collecting better evidence about what works best, and establishing a culture where this evidence is used as a matter of routine… Medicine has leapt forward with evidence based practice… I want to persuade you that this revolution could – and should – happen in education.**

Goldacre's clarion call to revolution echoes Slavin's from 11 years earlier in a way that suggests we may not have made much progress in the interim and that we still need to get over the threshold of convincing people. Similarly, 20 years after Hargreaves' speech, the 2016 White Paper reads as if we are just starting out.

What could possibly account for this lack of progress in the face of such obvious arguments in favour of evidence-based teaching? One recurring line of argument from its proponents is the inadequacy of the education community. Gorard and Torgerson (2006, pp 5–6) note that:

> **Antagonism to science (really just a synonym for research) is growing in HE… covered by the pretence of these individuals that they are being social scientists. Such pretend social science is overly concerned with social theory and all of the post- and -ism terms… and nebulous buzzwords… it may fool students and those responsible for funding, and thus undercut… the efforts of those trying to do better.**

For others, the shortcomings lie with the community of school teachers. For example, Hargreaves (1996, p 4) states that:

**For a teacher to cite research in a staffroom conversation about a pupil would almost certainly indicate that he or she was studying for a part time higher degree in education or rehearsing for an OFSTED visit – and would be regarded by most colleagues as showing off.**

If we accept this line of argument, it seems that we can only conclude that evidence-based teaching has not taken hold during the last 20 years because the education community is especially perverse or in some way inadequate. More inadequate than 'primary school children' and puzzlingly more perverse than the professional communities of medicine, agriculture, transportation and technology, which Slavin (2002) cites as areas where evidence-based practice has resulted in revolutionary progress.

If we see no reason why educators as a community should be more inadequate or more wilfully perverse than other professional communities, then we have to look for alternative explanations for why so little progress has apparently been made with what seems, to proponents of evidence-based teaching, obvious. Among these alternative explanations are those that say:

• Evidence-based practice does not work in education like it does in other areas (it is interesting to note that technological areas dominate Slavin's list and medicine is the usual comparison).

• Evidence-based practice will work but that the wrong models have so far been tried.

• This is a capacity issue; teachers do not have the time and have not had the opportunity to develop the skills necessary for evidence-based practice.

In relation to the second and third bullet points, it is worth noting from the timeline that different publications from various organisations have stressed alternative aspects of evidence-based teaching. For example, the 2016 White Paper emphasises the role of the EEF in providing easily accessible and understandable reviews of research findings, whereas the BERA-RSA report emphasises the importance of time and capacity for teachers' research. So not everybody necessarily agrees on what the best way forward might be.

It is also worth noting from the timeline that some ideas have been tried more than once. For example, the EPPI-Centre was funded in 2000 by the government to provide an online collection of reviews of research. This was no longer updated after 2007 and made little appreciable impact on work in schools. However, the EEF now has a similar role (about to be expanded). Will it work this time and, if so, why?

The point of these observations about the recent history of advocacy for evidence-based teaching is not to try to debunk it. It is rather to suggest that it is important to take the long view so that this can inform our efforts in the present. It is important that we do not underestimate the challenges of establishing evidence-based teaching and that we do not identify the wrong obstacles to making progress. This is particularly important for many young and energetic teachers who may not know the longer history and may find it easy to be convinced by the plausible rhetoric of more recent advocacy that this is indeed a 'no brainer' that will deliver unarguable gains in a straightforward way.

## 1.5 The main lines of argument from both proponents and opponents of evidence-based teaching

In the dialogue below, the arguments for evidence-based teaching are situated to the left of the page with counterarguments situated to the right.

**Most education research carried out has no impact on teaching in schools. This is because education research carried out in universities is irrelevant to schools. It is too small scale, it is not cumulative and it is based on unreliable data and researcher bias. What is needed is more studies of 'what works' based on questions relevant to teachers. Educational practice in schools is based on fad, fashion, personal preference and tradition rather than robust evidence.**

(Hargreaves, 1996; Tooley and Darby, 1998; Davies, 1999; Slavin, 2002; Hillage et al, 1998; Gorard and Torgerson, 2006)

**Studies of 'what works' are not enough for education as many of the important decisions in education are made on the basis of values. The risk of 'what works' studies is that they assume we already know what outcomes are desirable for education and that we don't need to explore any further what we think the purpose of education is and what values we should be operating by. This is also an important part of education research. Evidence-based teaching could be a way of using supposedly neutral scientific methods to marginalise democratic control of educational values and practices.**

(Atkinson, 2000; Elliott, 2001; Biesta, 2007)

> But areas like medicine have made much more progress than education has. This is because they have adopted the use of RCTs and systematic literature reviews for research. This means they have a robust idea of what is scientifically proven to work. It is also because they have made these easily accessible to doctors.

(Evans and Benefield, 2001; Slavin, 2002)

> And on the topic of democracy – an evidence based approach might be more democratic as far as pupils and parents are concerned as it removes the bias and self-interest of the education profession from what happens in education.

(Oakley, 2001, 2002)

> RCTs are quantitative studies based on counting things that are easily measurable. They are also underpinned by a positivist world view that believes that there is only one version of the truth and that, with the right method, we can find out what it is. This might work for scientific areas like medicine but it won't work in education. Firstly, because not everything we are trying to achieve is easily countable (eg developing character, resilience, values etc). Secondly, because education is not causal like medicine. A drug might be able to cause a recovery but you can't cause learning in the same way. Pupils have free will and have to want to learn. Finally, because the social world is more complex, diverse and unpredictable than the physical world. One immunisation might cure all small pox but one teaching method can't work with all pupils in all schools.

(Hammersley, 1997; Clegg, 2005; Biesta, 2007; Gale, 2018)

Arguments like the last one show a lack of understanding of the reality of medical research and practice. Doctors deal with more than just which medications or other interventions work in RCT conditions. The world of medical practice is every bit as socially complex as the world of education and has to take the same account of patients' individual histories, culture, identities, subjective perceptions and so on. Medical research also covers these issues. Medical practice is a sophisticated interplay between 'what works' in RCTs and understanding how to apply this in the complexity of specific personal and social circumstances.

(Hargreaves, 1996)

Also, RCTs and systematic reviews were used in education before they were used in most other areas. The earliest are from the 1930s and they are actually less problematic in education than they are in medicine.

(Davies, 1999; Oakley, 2002; Torgerson et al, 2005)

The fact remains that education is still predominantly a practical not technical profession. This means that the 'engineering' model of the relationship between research and practice will not work. It isn't possible to take a generalised research finding and apply it directly to changing practice in a 'quick fix' way. Successful education relies on specific local factors such as a good understanding of, and relationship with, your particular pupils. The risk of RCT and systematic literature review models is that they will become, in reality, a way of imposing standardised practice on teachers with no regard for their local expertise. It will just become part of the government's accountability agenda and the continued deskilling of teachers.

(Hammersley, 1997; Atkinson, 2000; Biesta, 2007)

> And by the way, you are right that the idea that large scale 'scientific' education research could inform practice was tried in education decades ago. It was the failure of that work to be useful to practice that led to the type of education research we have today. So what you are suggesting is not a step forward but a step backwards.

(Hargreaves, 1996; Hammersley, 1997)

> One of the reasons that RCTS were abandoned in education is because they showed that approaches that were popular didn't actually work. So the education community decided to 'shoot the messenger' of RCTs rather than accept the message.

(Torgerson, 2001)

> Also, if you look at the medical model again you will find that doctors have a lot of personal latitude in terms of what they do. Some people suggest that it is more accurate to say that their practice is 'evidence-informed' rather than 'evidence-based'. They take account of the RCT and review evidence but they also use their own experience, clinical judgments and patient preferences to decide how to act in specific circumstances. Teachers also make similar qualitative judgements about how their pupils learn that help us understand causal mechanisms and processes and why they have occurred.

(Hargreaves, 1997; Davies, 1999; Connolly, 2018)

> That's all very well but they are doctors and not teachers. Culturally they have more status and institutionally they have more independence from government prescription. You can't separate ideas like evidence-based teaching from the specific political, cultural, historical and institutional context in which they are put forward. In the last few decades government has increased its control over education right down to prescribing specific classroom practices. This is what will happen with evidence-based teaching. Supposed evidence will be used to make government political decisions about education look as if they are just based on unarguable facts.

(Atkinson, 2000; Elliott, 2001; Clegg, 2005)

You're right about rampant government prescription, but think about it this way: how much of that government prescription is based on robust evidence? And after having imposed a particular strategy nationally how robust is the evaluation of its effectiveness? You should welcome robust evidence-based practice in education as a way of making sure governments can't impose ideas for ideological reasons or without a basis in sound evidence (the same is true of some of the 'solutions' peddled by education companies). In practice, it should be fine for individual teachers to act with the latitude of doctors taking account of personal experience and local circumstances as a counterbalance to the centrally reviewed research evidence. However, governments shouldn't be allowed to impose disruptive and expensive strategies without the evidence and without evaluating them robustly.

(Davies, 1999; Hargreaves, 1999; Torgerson, 2001)

Is it the case that government intends to expose itself to increased scrutiny rather than the teaching profession?
Aside from that, there are other fundamental problems with RCTs and systematic literature reviews that mean they are not as robust as claimed. Firstly RCTs only measure causality. Not everything it is worth knowing works on that model. For example, we might want to know about pupils' experiences of a particular aspect of schooling in their own words.

(Atkinson, 2000)

Agreed. RCTs are only one form of research and for some kinds of questions other forms of research might be more suitable. Systematic literature reviews can take into account and synthesise diverse types of research.

(Davies, 1999; Evans and Benefield, 2001; Torgerson, 2001; Slavin, 2002)

> But systematic literature reviews judge RCTs as the highest quality form of research and, therefore, give them greater priority over other types of research. Partly as a result of this, despite the rhetoric about robustness, actual examples of RCTs in education do not appear very robust at all. If you look at the systematic literature reviews on the EPPI-Centre website, they exclude so much research as of insufficient quality that the final conclusion of the reviews is often based on very little. However, they still offer conclusions, which mean that these conclusions are less robust than much other research. They also seem to assume that you can remove all the debate and argumentation from the research and extract only the data as if the rest didn't matter or was just a distraction from the numbers.

(Clegg, 2005; MacLure, 2005)

> This problem is created by the lack of RCTs in education which shows the depressing state of education research. If there were more RCTs in education research then the systematic literature reviews would be better and more useful.

(Torgerson et al, 2005)

> Does that beg the question? It seems to assume that we have already agreed that systematic literature reviews based on RCTs are the most robust form of research evidence. Whereas my argument is that they leave out so much that they are questionable anyway.

(Clegg, 2005; MacLure, 2005)

> Agreed. Systematic literature reviews still need some development to be fully appropriate to education but we can do that work rather than just rubbish the whole idea.

(Oakley, 2002; Oakley et al, 2003)

> Is there also a risk that the requirements of systematic literature reviews will drive research funders to only fund RCTs? Which means we will only find out the sort of things that RCTs can find out.

(MacLure, 2005)

> All forms of research are valuable and there is no reason why RCTs should become the only form.

(Hargreaves, 1996; Evans and Benefield, 2001; Slavin, 2002)

> One of the main arguments for the superiority of RCTs is their scale and the large numbers that they use This means that they are expensive and time consuming. As a result they can only be done with the support of large (and relatively wealthy) organisations. Does this mean that centrally funded research asking centrally funded questions will take priority over smaller scale local research, such as research done in one school?

(Torgerson, 2009; Wiliam, 2014)

> If you remember the example from medicine, you will see that it is possible for research at both levels to have value. Evidence from RCTs and systematic literature reviews can inform practice but questions of local applicability and local effects can be decided by smaller scale local research. So practice will be based on a diverse range and type of evidence.

(Davies, 1999)

> But, the current government approach seems to emphasise the centrally held repository of 'what works' rather than the local practitioner research. The experience of Teaching School Alliances is that it is difficult to get practitioner research to take hold because of constraints on time and limited research literacy among teachers. If we want evidence-based teaching to work we need to address these issues, particularly the time issue as without this the rest will be difficult to achieve. The EEF model seems to suggest that what are needed are quickly accessible, easily digestible ready-made answers because teachers have little time. What is actually needed is the time. Particularly as research on knowledge mobilisation and translational research argues that it is important to put time and effort into finding out how general findings relate to specific circumstances.

(DfE, 2016; Nelson and O'Beirne (NCTL), 2014; NFER, 2014)

> Practitioner research is valuable but 'bottom up' strategies would also benefit from more rigorous experimental evaluation.

(Hargreaves, 1998; Evans and Benefield, 2001)

These arguments are summarised below in the form of a Research Map which moves from the initial impetus (the catalyst) making a claim for the use of more evidence in education. This is followed by the key proponents making a critical response and those academics taking a more defensive approach. These positions then take us to onto contemporary debates around different possibilities for the use of evidence in education.

## 1.6  Research map

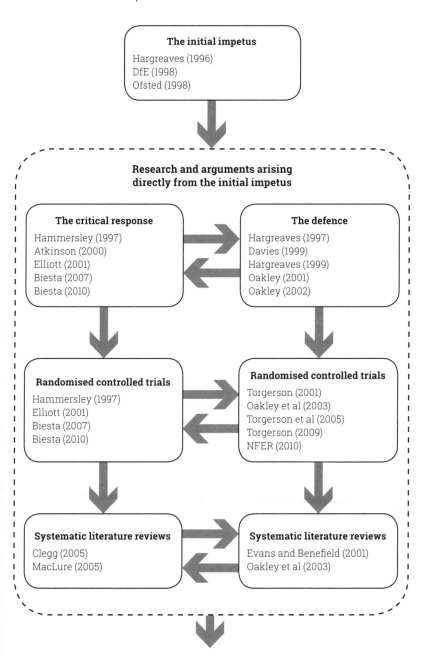

Research and arguments related to evidence in teaching
with a looser connection to the initial impetus

**Clinical practice models**

Hammersley (2005)
Biesta (2010)
Philpott (2017)

**Clinical practice models**

Alter and Coggshall (2009)
NCATE (2010)
Burn and Mutton (2014)

**Professional learning
communities/Rounds**

Bottery (2003)
Codd (2005)
Servage (2008)
Servage (2009)
Roegman and Riehl (2012)
Ellis and McNicholl (2015)
Roegman and Riehl (2015)

**Professional learning
communities/Rounds**

Dufour (2004)
Stoll et al (2006)
City et al (2009)
Roberts (2012)
Del Prete (2013)

**The contemporary debate**

**The renewed impetus**

Goldacre (2013)
DfE (2015)
DfE (2016a)
BERA, Baumfield and Mattick (2017)

**Teachers and research/
knowledge mobilisation/
translational research**

Hemsley-Brown and Sharp (2004)
Cooper et al (2009)
Furlong (BERA) (2014)
Nelson and O'Beirne (NFER) (2014)
Cain (2015a)
Cain (2015b)

## 1.7  Summary

Debates about evidence-based teaching have been raging in the education community for at least 20 years with no obvious signs of a widespread systemic change towards this approach. Unless we accept that the education community is especially inadequate or perverse, we must consider that the challenges are greater than some proponents would have us believe. The debate is less about whether teaching should be based on evidence and more about which type of evidence it should be based on, who should be producing that evidence and in what ways. It is also about how different types of evidence interact at the point of practice.

### Questions for enquiry in your own school

- Is the teaching in your school based on personal preference, tradition and/ or fads?

- How evidence-based/informed are whole school teaching and learning policies?

- How rigorous is your evidence of their success?

- What are the main challenges for evidence-based teaching in your school? Consider the following:

- teacher attitudes;

- access to research evidence;

- time to carry out practitioner inquiry;

- research literacy;

- something else.

- What is the best balance of ready-made solutions and practitioner enquiry for your school?

### Exploring further

For a slightly different perspective on the nature of evidence use in education we recommend you dip into this book:

Kvernbekk, T (2016) *Evidence-based Practice in Education: Functions of Evidence and Causal Presuppositions*. London; New York: Routledge.

Campbell Collaboration: www.campbellcollaboration.org

Centre for the Use of Research and Evidence in Education (CUREE): www.curee.co.uk

Education Endowment Foundation Teaching and Learning Toolkit: https://educationendowmentfoundation.org.uk/evidence/teaching-learning-toolkit

MESH Guides: www.meshguides.org

National Institute for Health and Care Excellence: www.nice.org.uk

The Evidence for Policy and Practice Information and Co-ordinating Centre (EPPI), University of London: https://eppi.ioe.ac.uk/cms

The Sutton Trust: www.suttontrust.com/research

What Works Centres: www.gov.uk/guidance/what-works-network

# Chapter 2
# Systematic literature reviews

## 2.1  Chapter overview

This chapter will outline:

2.2  an introduction and key ideas;

2.3  key debates about systematic literature reviews and implications for education;

2.4  practical steps you can take (connected to underlying principles);

2.5  a case study on evaluating success.

## 2.2  Introduction and key ideas

In Chapter 1 we concluded that while it might be important for teaching to be based on evidence, the *type* of evidence, *how* it is produced and by *whom* is of greater significance. While evidence as theory has its place in education, how it is translated into practice and how in turn practice may generate theory is another important consideration. In this chapter we turn our attention to assessing the quality of evidence and thinking about how existing literature, from a number of sources, can assist teachers in deciding 'what works' and what counts as good evidence (Biesta, 2007). In educational research, and especially for accredited graduate programmes (Undergraduate, Master's and Doctoral programmes), students are required to demonstrate, as far as possible, an unbiased account of the literature as it relates to their area of research. Put simply, does the literature review provide an unbiased picture of the views of other academics/authors and importantly what criteria has the author of the review used to provide a fair and balanced account of the field?

### What is a systematic literature review?

The evolution of systematic literature reviews has, over the past years, been in response to a lack of evidence-based accounts and especially within the field of medicine, where there have been conflicting accounts about, for example, different treatments (Bryman, 2016). In education and in social policy making, the use of evidence-based accounts is becoming more popular with decision-makers, often weighted around the quality and balance of evidence provided. The literature provides various terminologies for systematic review, including meta-analysis (this is mainly used to analyse quantitative research studies), research synthesis or systematic reviews. This is an academic response conflicting outcomes of many research studies, which is different from traditional or narrative literature reviews. These are largely based on the range and diversity of a large number of studies that have no clear audit trail or overt criteria as to their selection by the researcher (Oakley et al, 2005).

We saw in Chapter 1 that in 2000 the Department for Education and Skills (DfES) had funded the setting up of the EPPI-Centre at the University of London, which provided an online database of studies in health and education. There were significant challenges associated with this venture, especially as in education there are fewer scientific studies than were evidenced in the field of health. Most of the educational research consisted of small-scale qualitative studies, which made it a challenge to assess the methodological soundness of the research, how well the aim of the study related to the question posed in the systematic review, and the appropriateness of the study to warrant its inclusion in the systematic review.

To illustrate, Oakley et al (2005, p 18) provide an example of one such study which was conducted in 2003 by Philippa Cordingley:

The study focused on teachers of the 5–16 age groups and following a review of the literature on the impact of teaching and learning on sustained, collaborative continuing professional development (CPD), posed two questions:

1. Whether CPD has an impact on teaching and learning, and if so,

2. How is this impact realised?

The searching of electronic databases revealed 13,479 citations. 52 studies (1%) were relevant to the first stage of the review (question 1). Seventeen of these studies were included in the in-depth stage of the review. The criteria for this stage provided information about the impact on teacher practice and student learning and a set of quality criteria for study design and reporting (clearly stated aims, clear learning objectives for teachers, clear description of context and methods, evidence of attempts to establish reliability and validity of data analysis methods). Of these studies, the authors reported some positive aspects of teaching and/or learning outcomes and/or processes. No studies contributed to the 'whether' question and only one was judged to meet the 'how' question. The evidence therefore for the impact of CPD on teaching and learning was considered to be 'thin'.

There are three key areas for a systematic review:

1. What is the focus of the review: its purpose and scope?

2. What studies are relevant to the focus of the review?

3. How relevant is each study under consideration for the research question itself?

Looking at questions 1–3 from the perspective of a teacher who is keen to research an element of their practice, this first necessitates having a clear focus on what the research is about. Arguably, devising a quality research question before any reading has taken place is a challenge, but not impossible. In reality, the refining of a good research question (or research aim) takes place as knowledge of the subject under study is accumulated through reading. Secondly, a list of key words from the research question needs to be drawn up to provide a basis on which to search the literature. There are many types of literature to take into account: academic and professional texts, academic and professional papers (some peer-reviewed) and the 'grey literature' such as reports and conference papers. The third and final stage is reducing the vast number of papers, articles and so forth to include in the literature review. This is done by assessing studies which provide the best 'fit' with the research question, usually achieved by reading the abstract and including those that resonate with the aim of the research. It may also be appropriate at this early stage to think about which studies are outdated, and those which are seminal (for example, the work of Piaget is still relevant to education today). In addition, there needs to be a consideration of the contribution of the chosen literature to the knowledge-base and our increasing understanding of a particular educational issue and finally what recent literature is saying about the topic in question.

It is important to think about the criteria that will decide whether a study is accepted or rejected for review. Such criteria could include:

- Were the aims of the study clear (what type of data were collected, from whom, when and how)?

- What research methods were deployed and did they relate to the research aims?

- What theoretical constructs were used to drive data analysis?

- Was all of the above done systematically?

- Were the conclusions of the study in question based on sufficient quality data and were they warranted?

## 2.3 Key debates about systematic literature reviews and implications for education

The origins of systematic review emanate from health, following Archie Cochrane's challenge to medicine in 1972 in his book *Effectiveness and Efficiency*

(Oakley et al, 2005). His view was that the medical discipline had failed to organise its knowledge, and quality of care was often experienced as chaotic, ineffectual and sometimes harmful. In 2003 the Cochran Collaboration was established, whose overarching methodological approach was to provide an unbiased comparison of different interventions (Randomised Controlled Trials – RCTs – see Chapter 3) and the systematic collection of outcomes of different studies to establish the most reliable outcomes of bio-medical interventions. The practice of systematic review is now beginning to move into other areas such as social policy, which includes education policy. The key debate about systematic literature review is about 'fitness for purpose'. Is a more scientific type of approach a better 'fit' for education as some might argue (Evans and Benefield, 2001; Oakley, 2003, Oakley et al, 2005), or reliance on professional teacher judgements which have a focus on the practice of teaching (MacLure, 2005; Hammersley, 2001)?

More recently, the use of systematic reviews in education is predicated on the meta-analysis approach deemed as suitable for medical research involving RCTs (see Goldacre, 2013). Evans and Benefield (2001) and Oakley (2003) argue that much of the research conducted into classroom effectiveness and 'what works' is largely based on teachers' craft knowledge and less on robust research evidence that provides quality data for demonstrable impact on advancing knowledge about teaching and learning. Citing Davies (1999, p 109), Oakley (2003) notes that there are two levels of 'evidence-based education': the *use* of educational research and the *establishment* of sound academic research that pays attention to issues of scientific validity and practice relevance. Generating such knowledge from research requires:

- asking research questions that can be answered using empirical data;

- linking research to relevant theory;

- using methods that allow investigation of the research question;

- providing a chain of reasoning;

- replicating and generalising across studies;

- opening up research to professional scrutiny and critique.

This list, it is argued, provides the means to produce an objective judgement about the quality of articles and the criteria on which they are either accepted or rejected from the systematic review. The transparency of the methods used to source literature is predicated on copious descriptions of search terms used, from which databases they were sourced, and details of the filters used to select certain studies and reject others.

The scientific model of evaluating the worth of research studies is related to specific questions about 'what works' and underpins evidence-based policy making and practice (Hammersley, 2001). The 'evidenced-informed movement' associated with the work of the EPPI-Centre may be viewed as an audit-type culture whereby data-extraction, mapping, scanning and synthesis of information is the only way to produce quality evidence. The specific procedures for mining research papers for evidence alone privilege certain types of evidence while discounting others. In narrative or academic ways of reviewing literature, the actions of reading, writing and interpretation allow for tacit knowledge, expertise, dialogic interactions between researcher and other literature, and the generation of new ideas and ways of thinking that are not taken into account in systematic review (Dimmock, 2016).

Hammersley (2001), in a riposte to Evans and Benefield (2001), asserts that the actions of undertaking positivistic or scientific research should not be privileged over the academic-narrative approach to systematic review. MacLure (2005, p 398) agrees, suggesting that systematic review can '...*set limits on the ways that the world can be viewed and construed, and establishes what will count as truth'*. There is always an element of interpretation even when deploying systematic review, as following specific criteria or rules requires a form of judgement to be made. As far as policy making and the funding of educational research is concerned, if systematic review as a methodology is privileged above qualitative studies and is to be regarded as the 'gold standard', then only studies that answer single policy or practice questions will be used, which serves to ignore the processes involved in the implementation of policies (for example at the school level). The worth of qualitative studies lies *'with the processes involved in the implementation of policies, which are often not those assumed by policy-makers, and with unintended and unforeseen consequences'* (Hammersley, 2001, p 549). He goes on further to say:

**Rather, it [the review of the literature] can involve judging the validity of the findings and conclusions of particular studies and thinking about how these relate to one another, and how their interrelations can be used to illuminate the field under investigation. This will require the reviewer to draw on his or her tacit knowledge, derived from experience, and to *think* about the substantive and methodological issues, not just to apply replicable procedures.**

(Hammersley, 2001, p 549)

Systematic review is about accountability and the weighing of the 'evidence pig' to determine what quality is and what it is not. In education, national policies deploy similar approaches that lean towards prescriptive vocabularies which endeavour to promote conformity with the end users. There is an element of regulation (think about Ofsted and the tone of the inspection reports): a particular Ofsted 'house style', which may be thought of as restrictive, as the evidence collected during inspection might be contested by teacher professionals.

**Carrying out a qualitative review of the literature**

While quantitative evidence synthesis allows us to determine what might work and why, qualitative synthesis provides a means of exploring what works and why at a deeper level and draws very often on the perspectives of participants. It considers the context of the research as a background to the study and very often the lived experiences of the participants. It generally adds narrative to understanding a particular issue and while it does not lead to formulation of any laws (as might be evidenced with a meta-analysis or any scientific research), it does allow for some generalisation or transferability of findings that help to consolidate our learning about outcomes of research studies.

While qualitative researchers carry out a defined sequence of research 'steps', which consider issues relating to research ethics, a particular methodology which deploys a justified approach or method, the outcomes of the findings tend to be more open to interpretation. Put simply, quantitative researchers follow a series of pre-defined steps that is recognisable to that research community; qualitative researchers have more freedom to determine a particular approach to research or to consider a variety of ways in which to analyse their data. There tend to be no right or wrong answers with qualitative research; findings are open to interpretation by those who engage with the research. This approach enables the researcher to produce a rich evidence-base of data that can be reflected upon and discussed at length with interested others.

## 2.4  Practical steps you can take (connected to underlying principles)

Evidence-based approaches to teaching are gaining in popularity, particularly as schools are charged with using quantitative assessment mechanisms to determine the efficiency of student progress. There are many pre-determined and measurable outcomes that are open to public scrutiny and which provide quality indicators for how well a school is performing against national standards. Teachers need to be able to incorporate this 'hard data' into their work along with their 'softer' professional judgements made about progress of student learning. So what are the advantages of using a form of systematic literature review and how might this be possible given teacher constraints such as time and access to quality literature?

The reality for many teachers is that they do not have access to university libraries and therefore have to draw on texts they purchase, or websites that have open access to academic papers such as Google Scholar. However, there are many open access repositories freely available online that can provide useful information on different topics. Crucially, good research outcomes depend upon some initial preparation that helps to develop a good quality research question and a protocol to give direction to the research methodology. Table 2a outlines these steps and considers why it is important for researchers to follow them:

**Table 2a Key actions in preparing for systematic review**

| Key action | Why is this important? / What is important? |
|---|---|
| Identify your research topic | It is important that you are interested in the topic for your research but it may be limited by school requirements or funding that has been awarded, eg as part of a bidding process. Consider how much information there is already published in and around your areas of interest; it is a challenge to systematically review limited research on your topic. |
| Conduct a scoping exercise | A scoping exercise allows you to conduct a preliminary literature search in order for you to assess the quantity of available information already published on your research topic. In researching professional practice you may find either too much or too little information and you might want to re-review your initial area of interest. This exercise will also inform your research question. |
| Develop a focused research question | A focused research question gives your research a destination and a location you can return to when things become overwhelming or confused. The scoping exercise should provide a map of the literature in your field of interest and you may want to refine your research question at this point. |

| Key action | Why is this important? / What is important? |
|---|---|
| Talk to others about your proposed research | Garnering the views of other professionals and/or academics is a useful strategy at this point to rehearse your research question. Other perspectives will give you a range of different views on your proposal and can be used to further inform your research question. |
| Use your research question as a formal statement of the intention of your systematic review | The research question is an important driver of the research and always ends with a question mark. The question is usually a 'wh' question: What, Why, Where, How? Research questions should be focused and may require some refining in line with ideas coming from the literature review. |
| Develop inclusion criteria | Inclusion or eligibility criteria are developed in tandem with your research question and describe the specific elements of the research study. The Who, What, How and Where questions allow you to address specifically Who takes part in the research, What elements of the research need to be more fully defined, How will specific data be collected and Where will the research take place? |
| Design a review protocol | This provides a map of your research and subsequent research activities and helps you reach your research destination – in other words, it allows you to answer your research question. The protocol should include the current evidence-base, the research question and the methods you will use to answer the research question. |

The final stage of this preparation culminates in developing a search strategy. This is a term used to describe the methods you deploy to source the evidence you need to populate your research or literature review (Boland et al, 2014). In professional settings you may not, as already noted earlier, have access to a university library unless you are registered for a higher degree. If that is the case then you have a repository of information at your fingertips and the assistance of knowledgeable librarians who will be able to assist you further with searching relevant databases. For those not in a position to access a university library, the search strategy remains the same and requires a series of steps that demonstrates a sequential methodology for sourcing evidence.

**Table 2b Important steps in a search strategy (after Boland et al, 2014, p 39)**

| Step 1 | Consider what information is available to you |
|--------|-----------------------------------------------|
| Step 2 | List the sources you will search and keep a note of them |
| Step 3 | List key search terms (keep in mind your research question) |
| Step 4 | Outline your plans for minimising bias (your research outcomes should be trustworthy) |
| Step 5 | Consider how you will store and save your search results (password protected?) |

**Beginning your search**

We are all familiar with searching the internet and the use of search terms to access (usually) a plethora of information on a particular topic. Devising keywords is an important search strategy and in academic papers authors are charged with providing a keyword list to enable reviewers to access their papers more readily. The origin of keywords comes from your research question:

*Research title*

'The self-improving primary school': understanding and approaching teacher inquiry: a pilot study.

*Keywords*

Teacher inquiry; evidenced-based teaching; networking; knowledge; dissemination.

You should be prepared to play around with a number of keywords and closely related phrases to use in search engines, but do bear in mind you may have to search through many sources so try and be specific in this part of the search.

Bibliographic databases such as ERIC (Education Resource Information Centre) provide access to 1.5 million bibliographic records and are hosted by EBSCO (Elton B. Stephens Co), which provides a range of library database services. These databases allow you to conduct a more focused search because the search field has many search boxes which can be combined and function using Boolean operators 'AND', 'OR', 'NOT'.

'AND' narrows your search and returns references containing all of the search terms (teaching AND learning), 'OR' broadens the search (teaching OR learning), 'NOT' limits the search and retrieves references excluding education (teaching NOT learning).

Much of the literature you may come across in an internet search relate to reports, conference presentations and academic papers not listed in bibliographic databases. These publications form 'grey literature' but are still worth searching as they can provide up-to-date information. However, much of this body of literature is not peer-reviewed and so should be treated with caution.

You will also retrieve a substantial number of articles which are international although most are published in English. If your study is about UK schools for instance, then restrict your search to the UK and English-language only returns. Specifying a date range, say from 2000–2018, may help to reduce the number of returns. Be aware that seminal papers (those written much earlier but still relevant today) will not appear in your search.

Undertaking any review, whether systematic or narrative (academic), requires time and practice. Many of the returns will fall outside your chosen area of interest and you need to keep adapting your keywords and search terms for different search engines. From a bias perspective be aware that many studies report positive outcomes in order to be publishable, so you need to develop a critical eye and weigh up all the evidence on the issue before accepting the worth of such outcomes.

When you have completed your search it is time to think about which studies will be excluded from your search and how you will store those that remain. There are bibliographic software packages such as EndNote (www.adeptscience. co.uk/products/refman/endnote or RefWorks (www.youtube.com/user/ ProQuestRefWorks) that allow you to import citations from databases and the internet, but these are only recommended if you are attempting a very wide search (as in the preparation of a doctoral thesis). The first step is to identify any duplicate material (EndNote and RefWorks will identify any of these) and to remove them from the search. The next step involves thinking closely about what inclusion criteria you will use to identify eligible studies from your list of abstracts. Go back to your research question and list inclusion and exclusion criteria, as shown in Table 2c.

**Table 2c Selection of inclusion/exclusion criteria**

**Research title:**

'The self-improving primary school': understanding and approaching teacher inquiry: a pilot study.

| Must include | Must exclude |
|---|---|
| Primary schools: | Secondary schools |
| Mainstream | Further education colleges |
| Independent | Universities |
| Special schools | |
| Teacher inquiry | |
| Teacher enquiry | |
| Teacher research | |
| **May include** | **May exclude** |
| School improvement | School effectiveness |
| Ofsted | |
| Inspectorate | |
| Evidence-based teaching | Randomised controlled trials |
| Pilot studies with teachers | University pilot studies |
| School-university partnerships | |

## 2.5 Evaluating success

**Case study**

Jacqui and Alison were both Key Stage 2 teachers working with Year 3 classes. There had been a recent change in the national curriculum, meaning that children were required to be confident with more technical vocabulary and be able to independently apply these words to their work. Many children lacked a basic understanding of grammatical issues, so to help facilitate learning the children were divided into ability groupings and Jacqui and Alison considered some research (inquiry) type questions that focused on their teaching:

1. How should the work of the children be differentiated?

2. What teaching strategies are most effective for teaching grammar?

3. What literature might help us to understand this issue better?

Following a period of discussion between themselves and other teachers in the school, they realised that this problem was not just affecting Year 3 children but was common in other year groups in Key Stage 2. Professionally, their experience told them that generally speaking the use of colours helped children to organise their work more effectively and particularly so for children with Special Educational Needs. They decided to undertake some more robust research to see if their 'professional hunches' were correct. During an internet search and with particular focus on SEN, particularly dyslexia, they discovered a range of academic articles and websites that recommended using colour to help with not just organisation but also memory. It was important that the children developed memory 'muscle' to help them remember the meaning of grammatical terms and how they could be used. Jacqui and Alison also discovered in their search that rhyme and song would also help with memory and aid retention of information.

After collecting many sources they focused on the ones that should be included in their inquiry study, which resulted in many websites and a few academic papers. They eventually decided on the use of Grammaropolis (www.grammaropolis.com) as a way of educating the children to better understand how to use grammar. The inquiry was a great success and colour-coded writing was shared with the whole school and was eventually published (Trowsdale and Richardson, 2017). Using sequential strategies for a literature review (in this case more narrative than systematic) serves to:

- establish that there is a gap in professional knowledge;

- equip teachers with more knowledge about the subject;

- change thinking about a particular problem;

- widen professional knowledge production;

- change and improve teachers' practice;

- provide a platform for teachers to share and publish their work.

## 2.6  Summary

A systematic literature review is a way of locating, evaluating and analysing data that will provide the best quality evidence to answer a specific research question. Originally drawn from a bio/medical context, but now informing socio-economic government policy including education, systematic review of evidence follows a series of agreed well-defined and transparent steps that respond to the research focus, provide a critical assessment of the available evidence in the field under study and draw relevant conclusions around 'what works'. Systematic review has been privileged as the 'gold standard' of research approaches but fails to take into account a growing body of evidence that is premised on a less rigid model of research that considers a wider narrative or qualitative stance. While qualitative researchers often follow similar research steps to quantitative approaches (such as having a pre-defined research focus, a clear research question, a clear methodological approach), the research is generally less prescriptive than scientific research. Qualitative researchers are required to justify their research approaches (especially with regard to methods used for example) and very often the work is highly contextualised and draws upon participants' views and values, and there are more flexible ways of analysing and interpreting the data.

Since the time of Lawrence Stenhouse (1975) there has been a call for more use of evidence in education to demonstrate what works and why. More recently, there has been a resurgence of interest in randomised controlled trials through the work of Goldacre (2013) using quasi-experimental approaches and the production of quantitative evidence that demonstrates improvements in teaching and learning. In response to this audit-type culture where statistics are privileged, it is argued, by Hammersley (2001) and others, that there is another type of truth. This truth resides in the tacit knowledge held by educators, the contextual factors that may influence the type of outcomes that help to explain the statistical data. Systematic literature review is a way of using a tried-and-tested means of selecting the most appropriate literature that will inform a study and answer a specific research question. Academic or narrative reviews similarly follow a series of agreed steps, but allow for findings to be widely generalisable to other contexts, rather than producing fixed laws as is the case with systematic reviews.

## Questions for enquiry in your own school

- Identify staff who are undertaking study at a higher level, such as a Master's or Doctoral degree, or think about your own undergraduate studies, especially if you were charged with conducting some research in school. Ask them (or reflect on your own experiences) about the following points:

- How and where did you locate information about your research study?

- As a practising teacher possibly not registered for a higher degree at university, where would you source this information now?

- How would you assess the quality of the literature you source?
- What criteria would help to evaluate the worth of particular studies or books?

• Thinking about the school improvement plan (SIP), are there any areas where more professional knowledge is needed to support on-going improvement work?

• What sources of information are available to staff (books, reports, URLs of frequently used websites located in school)? How is it organised/updated and by whom?

• What links do you have with your local university to be able to access a wider range of academic material?

## Exploring further

The useful websites listed below provide some useful follow-up material if you wish to undertake a detailed review of the literature in your particular field of education. If you do have access to a university database, another useful read detailing how a systematic literature review has been used to research collaborative teacher research is by Willegems et al (2017) Teachers and Pre-Service Teachers as Partners in Collaborative Teacher Research: A Systematic Literature Review. *Teaching and Teacher Education*, 64: 230–45.

## Useful websites

It is possible to conduct an internet search using a search engine such as Google, which will return a large number of sites. In order to ensure the quality and authenticity of the sources you should begin your search with some of the more tried-and-tested sites listed below. This is of course not an exhaustive list, as Jacqui and Alison discovered, but will allow you to access mainly peer-reviewed articles.

British Library: www.bl.uk. National library of the UK.

EBSCO: www.ebsco.com/products/research-databases/eric. Gateway to EBSCO and ERIC free trial.

EEF: https://educationendowmentfoundation.org.uk, Teaching and Learning Toolkit: https://educationendowmentfoundation.org.uk/resources/teaching-learning-toolkit. Includes a summary of the international evidence on teaching 5–16 year olds.

Educational research abstracts online: https://scholar.google.co.uk/scholar?q=
educational+research+abstracts+online&hl=en&as_sdt=0&as_vis=1&oi=
scholart&sa=X&ved=0ahUKEwiUl-nOhqLWAhVhKcAKHcjpBDEQgQMIKzAA.
Repository of a range of educational research abstracts of which some are
freely available.

Educational Research Abstracts online from Taylor & Francis: www.education-
arena.com/era. Repository of international education abstracts (subscription
required).

EPPI-Centre: https://eppi.ioe.ac.uk/cms. Information relating to systematic
review and use of research evidence.

Google Scholar: https://scholar.google.co.uk. Repository of academic papers.

Ingenta Connect: www.ingentaconnect.com. Large repository for scholarly
publications.

National Foundation for Educational Research (NFER): www.nfer.ac.uk/
publications/educational-research. Free access to some editorials.

University online repositories. For example, derby.openrepository.com. All
universities now have open repositories for access to a large database of
information.

# Chapter 3
# **Randomised controlled trials**

## 3.1  Chapter overview

This chapter will outline:

3.2   an introduction to randomised controlled trials (RCTs);

3.3   what a randomised controlled trial is;

3.4   the claimed advantages of RCTs for education;

3.5   the practical challenges of conducting RCTs in education;

3.6   the (theoretical rather than practical) arguments for and against using RCTs in education;

3.7   how you might use RCTs in your school.

## 3.2  Introduction

This chapter is not intended as a guide on how to conduct randomised controlled trials (RCTs). Instead it focuses on the debates around whether RCTs are a useful approach to generating evidence in education. In order to do this, some detail about the practical conduct of RCTs needs to be given. However, if after reading the chapter you decide that RCTS are useful and you want to go about conducting an RCT yourself, there are a number of how-to guides available, some of them free. Information about these is given at the end of the chapter.

## 3.3  What is a randomised controlled trial?

An RCT is a form of experiment that is designed to test the effectiveness of a particular educational intervention or 'treatment' by comparing it to a 'counter-factual' situation in which the intervention is not used. Typically this is done by creating two populations of pupils, one of which receives the intervention and one of which does not. It is central to the RCT design that pupils must be assigned to these populations randomly and not according to any other considerations. Random assignment can either be done individually (ie pupil by pupil) or by cluster (eg different classes or schools are assigned to one of the two populations with every pupil in that class or school either receiving the intervention or not). The value of the random assignment is that it can be assumed that all variables in the populations (eg gender, prior attainment, socio-economic background, ethnicity) will be equally distributed, so whatever differences in outcomes identified between the two groups after the intervention can be attributed to the intervention. RCTs are currently most commonly used in medical trials, particularly drug trials. However, their supporters argue that they were used in educational research before they were used in medicine and that they are easier to implement in education than they are in medicine.

## 3.4 What are the claimed advantages for RCTs in education?

Proponents of RCTs claim that they are the only form of educational research that can identify causality in educational interventions (Torgerson, 2001). So if we want to know whether something works or not, conducting an RCT may be the only way to tell beyond doubt. For this reason, the term 'gold standard' has become attached to RCTs by some of their proponents and this claim to superior status over other forms of educational research has become the focus of much debate. Among the claimed advantages of RCTs is that they can be used to prevent large-scale disruptive and expensive educational reforms being introduced without any evidence of their effectiveness. They are also seen as the solution to the perceived weakness of much current educational research which, it is argued, is often too small scale, too politically or theoretically biased or too obscure or inconclusive to be of any use for informing educational policy and teachers' practice (Torgerson, 2001).

## 3.5 What are the practical challenges of conducting RCTs in education?

Before considering the arguments on both sides about whether RCTs' claims to superiority in educational research are justified, it is worth considering some of the practical challenges in conducting RCTs in schools. In some cases the practical challenges overlap with issues that will also be explored in relation to debates about the validity of RCTs as a form of educational research. However, in this section the focus is primarily on the practical issues.

To be sure that the effects measured in RCTs are the result of the intervention rather than chance variations, the populations used for RCTs need to be large. Where cluster randomisation is used rather than individual randomisation, populations need to be even larger. This is because it is the number of clusters that needs to be counted rather than the overall number of pupils. For reasons explored below, educational RCTs use cluster randomisation more often than RCTs in, for example, medicine. This means that it can be difficult for individual schools to conduct meaningful RCTs and they are possibly best done by groups of schools. This potentially brings with it challenges of organisation and of securing commitment and participation from all parties. This, in turn, involves resource implications. Most RCTs are conducted by organisations with access to considerable resources.

One defining assumption of RCTs as a test of causality is that the two populations involved differ (when considered as a whole) only in terms of the intervention used. This brings a number of organisational challenges. Firstly, with cluster randomisation it is important that clusters on each side of the trial are not different in terms of any variable. This means if the clusters on each side are schools, they should not be schools whose intake differs in terms of, for example, socio-economic background, ethnicity, gender or prior academic attainment unless these differences are balanced equally across both sides. The same is true if the clusters are classes within single schools. Again, this can bring implications for the number of clusters needed and the scale of the RCT as a whole.

The reason that cluster randomisation is used in education RCTs more often than it is in some other areas is that educational 'treatments' are more often given to groups together than they are to individuals (unlike in medicine, where medication is given to individuals). For example, it is difficult in practical terms to teach half of a class in one way and the other half in another way. Notwithstanding the practical difficulty, trying to operate in this way would also bring about problems of contamination. Another assumption of RCTs is that only one of the two populations receives the intervention. If there is a chance that the intervention can 'leak' across both sides, this undermines the validity of the RCT (Torgersen, 2001). This kind of leakage can occur in a number of ways. It can occur with pupils who share experiences with one another. It can occur when a teacher teaches classes (clusters) on both sides of the RCT. It can occur when teachers talk to one another about what they are doing. If the intervention being trialled has a superficial appeal as something that might seem better than current practice, some parts of it can become adopted on the control (ie non-intervention) side of the RCT. These issues of contamination are another reason why randomisation by schools rather than by classes within schools might be needed in order to ensure a robust design.

RCTs across a number of schools bring particular organisational challenges. One of these is the consistency of the intervention across schools. How do we know that multiple teachers in multiple sites are carrying out the intervention in the same way? Does this mean that all teachers will need to be trained in the same way in the intervention before the RCT? How much training will they need? Who will monitor the fidelity of implementation? Once again this might have resource implications.

Another issue related to variations in teacher behaviour in an RCT is differing levels of commitment or enthusiasm on either side of the RCT. The possibility is that teachers implementing the intervention might be more energetic and committed as a result of doing something new. Similarly, pupils on the intervention side might be motivated by the novelty of the intervention or by the sense that they have been chosen for something interesting that is not being made available to others. This is an example of the Hawthorne effect (Hutchison and Styles, 2010; Goodwin et al, 2010). Conversely, teachers on the non-intervention side may not have this boost of renewed enthusiasm, or even be demotivated by being 'left out', as might pupils. This could mean that short-lived affective factors rather than the intervention itself are influencing results. This situation might also cause differential drop out in which teachers or schools on the control side decide they are going to change their practice and, thereby, leave the RCT.

Trying to avoid this brings some practical organisational issues; some are easier to address than others. Firstly, the possibility of differences in teacher and school attitudes is one reason why strict random assignment of groups to each side is necessary. Assigning volunteer teachers or schools to the intervention side and using non-volunteers as the control side will increase the risk that the most enthusiastic and committed teachers and schools will be overrepresented on the intervention side. Even after strict random allocation, issues regarding motivation and demotivation might still remain. In medical RCTs these affective issues are dealt with through the use of placebos and double blinding so that neither patients nor doctors know who is getting the treatment and who is not. This is much less common in education RCTs where normal current practice is usually used as the control condition (Dray et al, 2014). Alongside the intervention under test, a 'dummy' intervention could be used for the control group, with the specific purpose of 'double blinding' the RCT. The practical challenges of this in the school context are probably clear.

Double blinding is therefore a challenge for educational RCTs. However, it is not the only practical consideration in relation to blinding. The first of these relates to randomisation. Properly robust RCT allocations should be totally blind. This can be done by allocating each individual or cluster an anonymous identifier such as a number. Whoever is allocating should not know who the identifiers belong to. In some RCTs random allocation is carried out by someone not involved in the rest of the trial. Assessment of outcomes should also be blinded if the RCT is to be as robust as possible. This means that whoever assesses the outcomes of the intervention and control groups should not know who they are assessing or whether they were in the intervention or control group. Again, some RCTs use external assessors to meet this requirement.

Another practical consideration might be the technical expertise that is needed to plan and conduct RCTs. Some of this is about gaining an understanding of the organisational requirements of conducting a robust RCT (as outlined above) and some of it relates to the statistical expertise required to calculate necessary sample sizes, effect sizes etc. Admittedly, conducting any kind of educational research requires the development of expertise and the demands of RCTs may be no greater than any other. They should also be within the collective capability of school staff, with appropriate guidance and support. However, it is important not to underestimate the level of commitment and organisation that even a relatively small RCT requires if it is to be valid (Goodwin et al, 2010; Fleisch et al, 2017).

It might also be worth noting that a practical shortcoming of RCTs is that they cannot, by themselves, tell us the mechanism through which something works. So the results of an RCT might show that a particular classroom strategy in mathematics produces improved mathematics scores. However, it cannot tell us what the 'active ingredient' is. Which part of the strategy is having the effect and/or how? To discover this you would need to research into the reasons why teachers think the intervention is or is not working. Their narratives and professional judgements add another dimension to the research, providing a greater depth of knowledge about the issue under investigation than just the statistical evidence alone can provide. These practical drawbacks of not knowing which part of the intervention is having the effect and why will be discussed in the case studies below (Hutchison and Styles, 2010).

Proponents of RCTs seem keen to demonstrate that they are manageable within school contexts. This is probably because they suspect that some opponents of educational RCTs will use manageability arguments to rule them out. Part of the debate about manageability turns on how pragmatic rather than perfectionist we are about the conduct of RCTs. RCT proponents would probably counter some of the challenges outlined above by arguing, for example, that:

- Variations in fidelity of implementation are acceptable because they are a feature of the real-world conditions in which any educational approach has to operate.

- Some contamination is not a problem as long as the whole of the intervention is not replicated on both sides.

- If we are mostly interested in big effect sizes then populations do not have to be unmanageably large.

- Resource implications can be offset by sources of funding for school-based educational research or by working with partner universities.

- Even in some medical research it is not always necessary (at least in the short term) to know why something works, just that it does.

However, these arguments have led some critics of the RCT proponents to question whether such a pragmatic approach to RCTs undermines their claim to be a gold standard in educational research, if they ever were. It is these claims and counterclaims that the next section explores.

## 3.6 What are the arguments for and against using RCTs in education?

The following research map captures, in overview, different positions on the landscape in relation to the use of RCTs for education research. At the right-hand side of the map, moderate opponents of RCTs and moderate proponents of RCTs often seem to occupy similar territory. Where they differ might be in who or what they are arguing against. Moderate proponents of RCTs (see Figure 3a) also still seem to view RCTs as superior to other forms of research but recognise that other methods are needed to fill in the gaps left by RCTs. They can also claim that, while other research approaches have value, only RCTs can test causation. On the other hand, moderate opponents might deny any hierarchy in research methods that makes RCTs superior. They can also argue that other research methods are equally good for testing claims about causality. Figure 3a makes clear some of these different positions.

### Figure 3a Research map

| | |
|---|---|
| **Strong proponents**<br><br>Argue that RCTs are the 'gold standard' in education research and that other approaches to education research are of significantly less value<br>Torgerson (2001); Oakley et al (2005); Oates (2007); Goldacre (2013) | **Moderate opponents**<br><br>Argue that RCTs are useful for some research in education but disagree that they are intrinsically superior to other forms of education research<br>Goodman et al (2010); Hutchison and Styles (2010) |
| **Strong opponents**<br><br>Argue that RCTs are inappropriate for education research because they are based on assumptions about causation that might be true in medical research but that are not true in education<br>Hammersley (1997); Clegg (2005), Biesta (2007, 2010, 2017) | **Moderate proponents**<br><br>Argue that RCTs have unexploited value for education and should be used more often but recognise that other research methods can also be useful and necessary<br>Styles and Hutchison (2010); Torgerson and Torgerson (2013) |

Areas of social provision, such as medicine, have made great progress in finding out what works by using RCTs. This is not the case, however, in education where it is clear that much of the educational research undertaken to date has been ineffective. Educational research appears to lack both rigour and validity and is undermined by the theoretical and/or political biases of the researchers. As educational research has nothing to say about causality and seems to contribute nothing to our knowledge of what works, it is letting schools and teachers down. Goldacre (2013) maintains that RCTs are the gold standard for research because only this method can test claims about causality. It also means that the research is free from bias; it is a fair test (Torgerson, 2001).

RCTs work in medicine because of the type of causality they test. Although variable social factors and personal attitudes and preferences need to be taken into account in medical trials, the number of variables in education makes any causality more difficult to pin-point. Complicating variables such as gender, social class, ethnicity, identity and personal aspirations make the identification of causality much less certain and less reproducible across different educational contexts.

RCTs are uniquely placed to deal with the complexity of the educational world and some of the earliest RCTs were done/completed in the field of education not medicine. RCTs in education can in fact be quite simple to facilitate. As relatively large populations can be randomly divided, and because we can assume that all the complicating variables are equally present on each side, the difference made by the educational intervention can be readily identified.

Many large-scale RCTs in education have discovered more variations in outcomes within particular educational interventions. Recent programmes of RCTs in the USA have produced mostly negative results showing no significant difference, overall, between teaching and learning strategies but a lot of variation within them. Similarly, in the UK a study looking at the effects of a school-based intervention on the attitudes and knowledge of primary children regarding their environmental awareness concluded no significant difference in their RCT between the experimental and control groups (Goodwin et al, 2010). This suggests that the contingent factors in education (eg personality of the teacher, pupil–teacher relationships, motivation) are more important than specific strategies. Similar results have been found in the health professions in areas such as counselling, where it seems that the personality of the counsellor and the relationship established with the client is more important than the particular method of counselling used. These contingent factors are best researched using methods other than RCTs.

But even if there are significant variations within interventions and varying contingent factors, RCTs still perform the useful function of showing what aspects of the interventions have had, on balance, positive rather than negative effects. The fact that many RCTs have produced no conclusive results about what works is actually part of a bigger problem with RCTs. Although they claim to be able to test for causality, there is no way of finding out what, in any given intervention, has caused the outcomes they measure. Among other problems, this means we don't know whether another simpler intervention would have exactly the same outcomes (Hutchison and Styles, 2010).

Although RCTs are the only robust test for causality, they can't describe what it is about any given intervention that is beneficial or why the intervention was successful. For this reason, it can be useful to accompany RCTs with methods of qualitative research that can look more closely at the process of the intervention in order to understand how any successful intervention has worked.

Where RCTs are used, other research approaches are relegated to a secondary role. This hierarchy needs to be questioned. Firstly, the claim that RCTs are the gold standard for researching causality is questionable. Experienced researchers outside the field of education contest the notion that RCTs can produce certainty on causality. They also challenge the assumption that they are the only way to establish causality. Firstly, they argue that RCTs cannot reliably establish that particular interventions are the causes of outcomes as there may be many other variables operating throughout the intervention. The complex interplay between school systems and structures means large-scale RCTs (as related, say, to a policy change) are difficult to trial (Hutchison and Styles, 2010). It is also problematic to 'blind' the trial as is the case with drug trials (where neither patients nor doctors know who is receiving the drug under test or a placebo). Often the intervention group 'tries harder' (known as the Hawthorne effect). Secondly, they argue that causality can be established by many other research methods including qualitative ones (Hammersley, 1997; Clegg, 2005; Biesta, 2007). Other ways of establishing causality could be established through the use of observation study, but this would not establish causality.

It is worth noting that even in medicinal trials the causal relationship between smoking and lung cancer was not established by RCT. Indeed, it was through the analysis of patterns in epidemiological studies that this causation was identified. RCTs are used where we have a potential cause (eg an educational intervention) and we want to isolate what the effect is.

The relative merits of quantitative and qualitative research paradigms and their use in educational investigations is open to debate; and the notion of a hierarchy where the former is seen as the 'gold standard' should, perhaps, be challenged. Whichever research strategy is adopted, it is unlikely that the privileging of a single method will address perceived weaknesses in educational research. Rather, it is the level of rigour and the depth of criticality found within each methodology that will determine the strength and validity of the research.

The choice of research method will, of course, be determined by the type of information the researchers hope to discover, and this should be clear from the outset of the investigation. Over-reliance on the use of RCTs in educational research may limit the usefulness of the data generated as it may not be possible to gain sufficient insight into possible explanations of the issue if the information is presented in number format only.

The dominance of qualitative research has been problematic for educational practice. Much qualitative research has been small scale and further harmed by fragmentation brought about by a lack of clarity regarding methodological and theoretical standpoints and differing ideologies. It is often not possible to identify causes or to generate objectively verifiable cumulative knowledge that has characterised progress in the physical sciences and in areas such as medicine, engineering and agriculture.

The type of cumulative knowledge that typifies knowledge development in science and technology is not possible (or even desirable) in education. This is, in part, due to the importance of contingent factors in education where success may not be directly attributable to particular teaching methodologies. The fact that the world in which education operates is inherently unstable also needs to be taken into account. Unlike engineering research into, say, the properties of a substance, what we discover through educational research may not remain constant. Information gleaned through educational research will always need to be interpreted through the lens of ever-changing social conditions and societal mores; and, as educational research is often undertaken with the explicit goal of changing practice (rather than simply describing it), such aspects will always be important or paramount.

## 3.7  How might you use RCTs in your school?

The roll-out of the National Literacy Strategy is a good example of an initiative which was implemented in schools without being subject to rigorous trials. Oates (2007) claims that this lack of testing could have resulted in children being exposed to educational harm. In their evaluation of the strategy, Smith and Hardman (2000) found no difference in examination results between schools piloting the strategy and those who had not yet started to implement it. This might lead us to conclude that the strategy had no effect on examination results. However, it is not possible to conclude this from the study, as the schools were not randomly chosen.

RCTs can, of course, have a role in building localised knowledge. Hutchison and Styles (2010, p 9) give a short example of how, in education, an RCT can be implemented. Consider this abridged version of their case study:

**Case study**

A teacher is convinced that formal tuition in study skills would improve her school's examination results. She knows she would contaminate the trial if she divided her class and worked with one half as the control group and one half the experimental group. She manages to recruit other teachers to her study and so three classes form the control group and another three the experimental group. She judges that no formal consent is required from parents as this is within her normal realm of decision making. Standard internal examinations occur every term, so two sets of examinations, a term apart, are taken as before and after the interventions. She judges that improvement in examination performance may be the result of the new technique which she will now use with her own class as well as recommending to other teachers.

## Comments on this case study

There are some key points to consider before any form of RCT/quasi-experimental trials in schools can be implemented. These relate to a number of issues, notably ethics, risk, experimenter expectation and contamination.

Ethical consideration must form part of all research preparation but decisions need to be taken regarding the extent to which investigations and interventions can be described as 'normal professional practice'. There is likely to be some blurring of the line between what is concerned research (where ethical approval must be gained) and normal professional practice where, as in the case outlined above, ethical approval may not be thought necessary.

In school contexts, making others (especially the school leadership team) aware of the project, during the planning stages, would promote discussion on this aspect of the investigation and help to publicise the project further. Establishing links with a university academic would enable school-based staff to gain a wider perspective on ethical issues and how these may need to be taken into account. Denying access to proposed effective teaching and learning strategies for either the control group or experimental group can also be thought of as an ethical dilemma and needs careful consideration in the research planning phase.

It is difficult to maintain a blind trial in schools; while pupils might not know they have been assigned to a particular group, the teachers obviously will. If classes are divided into an experimental and control group then pupils may quickly realise which group they are in and 'contaminate' the other group (for example, by sharing information outside of lessons). Blind trails may be more easily achieved when working at whole school level, especially if the participating schools are geographically distant in location.

Biesta (2017, p 323) talks about 'what works' and 'what works for what'? The causal relationships described in scientific research do not exist in professional action scenarios as there are just too many variables to control (if that were indeed a possibility). The researcher or the teacher who, for example, intervenes, to improve learning is, of themselves, a subject as they are part of the action. In education it must be remembered that it is extremely unlikely that research undertaken in one classroom will never/ever be fully replicated in another.

Scientific evidence, however gained, cannot tell professionals how to act, and research findings need to be interpreted by teachers. Much successful classroom practice is predicated on their professional judgement and the extent of the influence of this should not be underestimated. Indeed, Biesta (2007, 2010, 2017) sees this as a central part of the act of being a professional. The use of quantitative data cannot be allowed to override professional judgement.

## 3.8 Summary

RCTs have gained attention because in disciplines such as medicine and engineering they are considered the 'gold standard' of research approaches. However, undertaking research in education poses a different set of challenges. Finding out 'what works' in education, with its many complex strands, means that professional judgement is likely to remain at the forefront of classroom practice. This may mean that the use of RCTs is less appropriate in education where it is the interpretation of qualitative data that is paramount.

Undertaking large-scale RCTs may not be appropriate (or even possible) in schools. Where policy makers choose to operate these at a strategic level, the limitations of such processes need to be acknowledged. Careful consideration of ethical issues, sampling, causality and contamination needs to form part of the research planning and these important aspects of research should be revisited throughout the investigation process.

### Questions for enquiry in your own school

- Identify the current interventions being used in your school.

- Which interventions/initiatives might be suitable to trial as a small RCT?

- Using the case study described above, how would you plan for an RCT approach? What issues would you need to consider and why?

### Exploring further

- Connolly, P, Biggart, A, Miller S, O'Hare, L and Thurston, A (2017) *Using Randomised Controlled Trials in Education*. London; Thousand Oaks; New Delhi; Singapore: Sage.

This book, published in conjunction with the British Educational Research Association (BERA), focuses on the methodologies and philosophy of RCTs, how to run them in schools and ways of collecting and analysing data.

- Childs, A and Menter, I (2018) *Mobilising Teacher Researchers: Challenging Educational Inequality*. London; New York: Routledge.

This book reports on lessons learnt from the 'Closing the Gap' project, which involved 650 schools in England and looked at ways of closing the attainment gap. Contributors include proponents of RCTs such as Paul Connolly and those who take a more critical view such as Trevor Gale.

- Churches, R and Dommett, E (2016) *Teacher-Led Research: Designing and Implementing Randomised Controlled Trials and Other Forms of Experimental Research.* Carmarthen: Crown House.

Aimed specifically at teachers to enable them to design, conduct and analyse their own classroom-based research to inform their practice. Step-by-step advice is given on how to conduct a randomised controlled trial, and how to statistically analyse, interpret and report the data.

## Useful websites

Michael Gove and Ben Goldacre advertise two new RCTs to raise school standards (2013): www.gov.uk/government/news/new-randomised-controlled-trials-will-drive-forward-evidence-based-research

A rejoinder to Ben Goldacre by Marc Smith of the Guardian newspaper about the value of RCTs (2013): www.theguardian.com/teacher-network/2013/mar/26/teachers-research-evidence-based-education

Randomised Trials in Education: An Introductory Handbook by Professors Torgerson and Torgerson of the University of York: https://v1.education endowmentfoundation.org.uk/uploads/pdf/Randomised_trials_in_education-revised250713.pdf

# Chapter 4
# **Translational research and knowledge mobilisation**

## 4.1  Chapter overview

This chapter will outline:

4.2  an introduction to and key ideas about the relationship between translational research and knowledge mobilisation;

4.3  what professional knowledge is in the school context;

4.4  models of knowledge mobilisation: translating research knowledge into practice knowledge;

4.5  routes for dissemination;

4.6  teachers engaging with research;

4.7  key debates about knowledge mobilisation and implications for education.

## 4.2 Introduction and key ideas

Raising educational attainment through improvement of teaching and learning has long been a long-term vision held internationally and showcased through much educational research and the UK inspectorate. Teachers do not routinely engage with outcomes of academic research and do not have the time or the access to university libraries to source and review the many papers published every year. The transfer and translation of knowledge from academic research to professional practitioners is known as knowledge mobilisation. The term 'translational research' refers to the way in which available research knowledge makes its way into professional use. The process by which this occurs is known as knowledge mobilisation (la Velle, 2015; Ovenden-Hope and la Velle, 2015). Practitioners may also argue that their professional experience and uniqueness of school setting makes engaging with empirical research a less meaningful experience. In the fast-paced world of teaching they prefer to rely on gaining more knowledge from their own workplace, professional events, professional publications and the media. The work of academics engaged in research is different from the work of teachers, and as a routine these two groups rarely meet to share the outcomes of their work. Where they do and where they engage in practitioner research together, there is a better opportunity for empirical knowledge to be collaboratively generated and valued by both groups (Hemsley-Brown and Sharp, 2003; Cordingley, 2008). Practitioners who themselves engage in research demonstrate an intellectual, practical and emotional engagement with the research and are more likely to value the quality of not only the knowledge they generate, but are more willing to disseminate and therefore transfer that knowledge to other practitioners (Levin, 2008).

As seen in previous chapters (and discussed in more depth in Chapter 7), clinical models have found favour more recently as a means of generating a wide body of evidence, such as through the use of RCTs (see Chapter 4 and the work of Goldacre, 2013). These have focused more recently on the methods of collecting data, such as randomised controlled trials and the use of evidence from systematic literature reviews which have achieved a 'gold standard' position (Campbell et al, 2017). There are those that challenge these new ways of thinking about educational excellence (Biesta, 2015, 2017; Campbell et al, 2017) suggests that our preoccupation with numbers is in some way eroding the democracy of teacher professionalism and that numbers themselves provide a means of seducing us into believing these measurements are the only ways in which we can judge whether our education system is effective. In a neo-liberal age where measurement and provision of evidence are taken as quality indicators of performance, the way in which practitioners make judgements about their professional actions can never be replicated by research. Biesta (2017) challenges the demand to work in an evidence-based way:

**...as an attempt to eradicate professional judgement with regard to the 'how' and the 'what for' of professional action from the domain of professionalism. It seeks to transform professions into abstract 'machines' in which reflection and judgement are seen as a weakness rather than as an essential part. This shows how the call for an evidence-based approach is not a deepening of the knowledge and judgement of professionals, but rather an attempt to overrule such knowledge and judgement. In precisely this sense, the evidence-based approach is another erosion of the democratic dimension of professionalism and hence another post-democratic distortion.**

While it is useful to acknowledge these debates, they do little to offer a solution to the age-old problem of getting teachers interested in research, a challenge that is likely to stem from the clear differences between school and university cultures. Research, for example, is often privileged in universities. Given the nature of teachers' daily work, this is not something that can be replicated in schools. In today's fast-paced ever-changing world of education, teachers are charged with making quick decisions, few of which can be based on good research evidence. Cain (2015b) suggests that teachers use research conceptually, which enables them to know what to think about and how to think. He suggests that through engagement in research and the increased opportunities to discuss aspects of their pedagogy, teachers are offered a third voice. Provision of the first and second voice comes from teachers and their colleagues, respectively. This experiential knowledge-base is a critical component of the evidence-base for teaching and an integral part of the knowledge-base. The ways in which this knowledge is mobilised for the use of decision-makers, practitioners and researchers assumes there is some degree of social interaction between these groups that promotes the co-creation of knowledge. This might be achieved individually but is more likely to occur through group work teacher networks and educational partnerships (Campbell et al, 2017, Prenger et al, 2017).

## 4.3 What is professional knowledge in the school context?

Over time, teachers extend their knowledge about teaching and learning through professional development. Eraut (1996, p 1) defined teacher knowledge as *'the knowledge possessed by professionals which allows them to perform professional tasks, roles and duties with quality'*. Table 4a illustrates Eraut's domain of teacher knowledge.

**Table 4a The domain of teachers' professional knowledge (Eraut, 1996, p 25)**

|  | Area of knowledge | | | |
|---|---|---|---|---|
| **Context of use** | Subject matter knowledge | Education knowledge | Situated knowledge | Societal knowledge |
| Classroom knowledge |  |  |  |  |
| Classroom-related knowledge |  |  |  |  |
| Management knowledge |  |  |  |  |
| Other professional roles |  |  |  |  |

These different forms of knowledge can be mapped along two dimensions, vertically for knowledge related to context and horizontally for knowledge related to specific areas of education as related to the education of children. Teachers will be required to draw upon different forms of knowledge, so while 'knowing how' is vital for professional work, 'knowing that' is a form of propositional knowledge gleaned from wider interaction with other professionals, reflection on action and experience (Day, 1999).

Today's teaching standards which are mandatory for all trainee teachers both during their training and during their initial years as Newly Qualified Teachers (NQTs) and Recently Qualified Teachers (RQTs) are premised on three factors: firstly, drawing upon the findings of research and scholarship that form the subject matter of the school curriculum (English, mathematics, history and so on); secondly, drawing upon bodies of knowledge such as sociology, psychology, philosophy; and thirdly, as Shulman (1987) concludes, the 'intuitive credibility' or 'face validity' that reflect the interests of the teaching profession and are mirrored in the education of novice teachers. Roughly translated, these three factors form a foundation of teaching skills that demonstrates interpersonal skills (such as good communication), knowledge of subject matter and an understanding of pedagogical skills.

Teachers have access to a body of knowledge which some might describe as 'good practice'. Much of it is codified and held in the heads of teachers; some is only accessible to certain groups of teachers (such as school leaders and managers) and other forms of knowledge are tacit or implicit (Polanyi, 1967). These are less easily explained by teachers. Teacher research or inquiry normally arises as the result of some classroom concern, and the ensuing research (possibly through action research processes) allows the teacher to gain knowledge about the issue under investigation. Primarily, this new knowledge belongs to the individual teacher, but when shared with others through professional relationships such knowledge is 'tested for truth', analysed, evaluated and, in many cases, added to the school repository of knowledge. The total content of knowledge held by any one school could be referred to as its 'intellectual capital' (Hargreaves and Fullan, 2012), and is a school that regularly audits, manages, validates and disseminates its new knowledge (Hargreaves, 1999).

In the current educational climate there is an ever-increasing demand for knowledge creation, as part of the ever-present ideology of school improvement. The de-centralised approach to education where the importance attached to partnership working, through the creation of alliances of schools and colleges and the development of networks in and between schools, is readily acknowledged, the responsibility for improvement is placed firmly with school-based management and teaching teams; and the creation and sharing of knowledge is an integral part of this process. School leaders are charged with shaping school culture to invest in and promote knowledge creation, knowledge sharing and knowledge dissemination. This includes having a keen awareness of the external environment, and an appetite for seeking opportunities to assimilate and exploit external knowledge. Teachers' practice is informed by intelligence gathered from many different quarters ranging from material gleaned from informal discussions with other colleagues in school to the more formalised information made available by school leaders, governors, parents, and the inspectorate. All of these elements have to be translated in some way before they can be become embedded in their practice. So as Cain (2015a, p 491) argues:

> **Education, therefore, cannot be based on research; there is too little overlap between what education needs, and research provides. The question is, whether research can contribute to educational practice at all.**

40 years later, this quote from Shulman (1987, p 6) still resonates:

> **When policy-makers have sought "research-based" definitions of good teaching to serve as the basis for teacher tests or systems of classroom observation, the lists of teacher behaviours that had been identified as effective in the empirical research were translated into the desirable competencies for classroom teachers... They were accorded legitimacy because they had been "confirmed by research". While the researchers understood the findings to be simplified and incomplete, the policy community accepted them as sufficient for the definitions of standards.**

Conceptualising the process of knowledge creation is a challenging task for school leaders. Hargreaves (1999), drawing on an industrial model of knowledge creation, postulates four modes of knowledge based on interactions between tacit and explicit knowledge:

1. Socialisation: on the job training, eg through a training programme, generates tacit knowledge;

2. Externalisation – collective reflection and dialogue turn tacit knowledge into explicit knowledge;

3. Internalisation – 'learning by doing' or gaining experience turns explicit knowledge gained in point 2 back into tacit knowledge;

4. Combination – a process of elaborating and sharing through networking forms of explicit knowledge with others.

(Hargreaves, 1999, p 127)

Validation of knowledge in teacher circles is commonly described as 'good (or best) practice', 'it worked for me', 'practice wisdom' and so on. This is a personal or *ipsative* judgement about what constitutes effectiveness in practice made on the basis of discussion and debate with other teachers. As such it is often only shared locally.

The knowledge-base of teaching is multi-layered and cannot be either fixed or final. The following brief list summarises the key areas of knowledge most commonly drawn upon by teachers:

- Knowledge of educational contexts, different school phases and types of school (maintained, independent, special schools); how schools are organised, governed, financed; and how they operate as part of wider communities of schools such as Teaching School Alliances, Multi-Academy Trusts.

- Knowledge of historical legislation that brought about key changes in the education landscape and the concomitant debates on the purpose and value of education today.

- Deep knowledge of subject content appropriate to a specific school age-phase and, perhaps in less depth, knowledge of school phases.

- Curriculum knowledge to teaching schemes, changes in curriculum and the assessment points throughout a child's education journey.

- Pedagogical content knowledge – 'how to teach' including classroom management skills in order to be able to effect learning and to demonstrate an understanding of the learners and their characteristics.

(Adapted from Shulman, 1987)

Much of the educational research over the years has not been able to document a history of evidence about what constitutes effective practice in teaching. Shulman (1987, p 11) describes this as 'individual and collective amnesia', and in comparison with other professions such as law, medicine and architecture, there is no single blue print for the codification of teaching or practice wisdom. Shulman compares this situation for educators with the undeveloped and less populated chemical periodic table available to natural philosophers over a century ago. As a result of research undertaken more recently, we have been able to populate education's equivalent to the periodic table and to expand the knowledge-base available to teachers.

There are, however, very specific differences between knowledge that is generated by academic research and the pedagogical/curriculum or 'school' knowledge that is respected by teachers. Academic research that is peer-reviewed by other academics and that has rigour and (in some cases) a degree of originality is valued by teachers for its significance. It has a specific focus, which is researched over a period of time and can be classed as propositional and theoretical knowledge. Conversely, pedagogical knowledge is valued by teachers as it often has direct practical application in the classroom. Such knowledge can have many foci and can be used to inform swift and fluent thinking. Much of it is context specific and based on professional and personal values (after Cain, 2015a).

## 4.4 Models of knowledge mobilisation: translating research knowledge into practice knowledge

Although the benefits of research have long been recognised by the likes of Stenhouse (1975), Shulman (1987) and, more recently, Hargreaves and Fullan (2012) and BERA-RSA (2014), there remains a broad divide between how research is undertaken by academics and how it is used by teachers to inform and guide schools in the development of policy and practice for the teaching profession. This schism means that translational research (the movement of research knowledge into actionable professional use) is not often encountered/ witnessed in schools. The intermediary agents and processes that enable the translation to be used in practice and inform policy (knowledge mobilisation) (la Velle, 2015) are, therefore, frequently under-used and often moribund.

At a simplistic level we need to understand how teachers might use their practice wisdom or codified teaching knowledge and how this can be translated for others to draw upon and use in their own practice. Teaching is a complex activity, and in order to succeed teachers need to develop sound subject and pedagogical knowledge (including knowledge of how to affect student behaviours) and to understand how this can be applied within internal and external frameworks. If teachers are to be transformative in relation to making substantive changes to their practice or ways of thinking about their practice, then they need to be collectively working towards school improvement, functioning as a teacher-researcher involved in teacher inquiry to gain new knowledge (Day, 2017). Simply telling teachers to change/adjust their practice is ineffective as they need to engage emotionally and intellectually with the process of change if they are to see the relevance of it (Segedin, 2017).

It is clear that teachers have a sense of their own knowledge, often held as personal theories of teaching which they may choose to espouse/share with others. Teachers who mentor teacher-trainees sometimes find it challenging to explain their practice to novice teachers as, for them, the art of teaching is something gained through experience; and, although this tacit knowledge is often observable in practice, it can be difficult for established teachers to articulate it to others. Where classroom practitioners are engaged in teacher inquiry, the process can be used as a vehicle for making the unknown 'known'; Figure 4a shows how this might be achieved.

**Figure 4a Model of knowledge, inquiry and practice for the reflective practitioner**

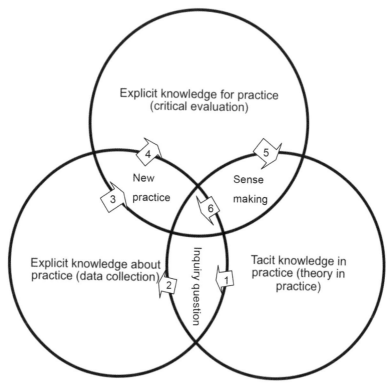

This diagram helps us to make sense of how teachers might generate and mobilise knowledge, through the use of research or inquiry. Follow the numbered arrows to learn more about each step:

1–2: Development of inquiry question on a particular area of interest presents the opportunity for some data collection.

2–3: Analysis and reflection on the data (evidence) turns tacit knowledge into explicit or actionable knowledge.

3–4: New evidence about a particular issue generates new teacher knowledge, which in turn can be verified by adoption of a new practice/pedagogy.

4–5: The dissemination of this new explicit knowledge will allow for critical evaluation by others.

5–6: The process of 'sense making' with other teachers through critical evaluation of the data/evidence is a good example of knowledge mobilisation and further opportunities for knowledge-making within a wider school context.

Hargreaves (1999, p 128) argues that knowledge validation in schools is in a 'primitive state', but Figure 4a provides us with a mechanism that might allow knowledge to be generated, validated and held up to teacher scrutiny. Schools adopting this type of approach will be able to generate 'Mode 2 knowledge' (practice knowledge or practice wisdom), along much the same lines as Stenhouse (1975) had in mind. The next step might be to engage with Mode 1 knowledge (academy or university knowledge) and to link this with Mode 2 knowledge (for practice). By its very nature, Mode 2 knowledge is highly contextualised and is practical in its generation and subsequent use (Rickinson et al, 2011). It is propositional in nature, just as with Mode 1 knowledge, and to some extent it is possible to interact/interweave both modes of knowledge, as evidenced by an increasing number of school-university partnerships (Day, 1999).

Transitional research processes help to forge the transition from academic research theory to school practice (often referred to as 'praxis'). How to ensure that academic research evidence is used in practice remains a challenge. Drawing on the work of Best and Holmes (2010), Campbell et al (2017, p 212) summarises three models for knowledge-to-action processes:

1. **Linear models**: one-way relationship to make available evidence from academic research accessible to practitioners.

2. **Relationship models**: as linear models but with a focus on relationship building between academic researchers and practitioners, with a view to the development and mobilisation of knowledge across the divide to promote the translation of theory into practice.

3. **Systems models**: looking at systems overall, identifying barriers to mobilising research and practice knowledge and builds/building a more complex network where interaction, co-creation and implementation of evidence can be secured.

## 4.5 Routes for dissemination

Teachers do not routinely engage with many forms of dissemination, as part of their normal professional practice, but if they are to be *consumers* of knowledge then they should also be *producers* of knowledge as part of their intellectual work. Day (1999), drawing on the work of Drucker, sees teachers as contributors of knowledge who have a responsibility to generate their own professional knowledge so that they become *'knowledge workers'* (Day, 1999, p 176). Establishing a means of peer review within and between schools is a recognised way of mobilising and sharing knowledge that has the added bonus of empowering teachers whose ability to engage in critical dialogue increases/deepens. These routes for dissemination provide the space and opportunity for teachers to build relationships and to promote their work as they develop their knowledge capacity. Engagement with an innovation hub and/or university partners presents further opportunity for teachers to contribute to written publications that will potentially reach much wider educational audiences (Poultney, 2017).

## Disseminating research

Dissemination of new knowledge or practice has not been strong in schools, nor has it been required practice. Reaching teachers through traditional academic publishing routes is often ineffectual and collaborative/interactive approaches more akin to networking present opportunities for teachers to disseminate their work more widely, outside of their own school (Segedin, 2017). As a starting point, the most common way of disseminating knowledge is the sharing of practice between individuals either within the school or externally. Some teachers, however, gain knowledge from reading research papers or professional texts.

Transposition of knowledge is the movement of knowledge from a different place or context. This transfer of knowledge may only work in a new context if the teacher is highly skilled; and it is often a disappointment to teachers that they cannot achieve the same level of success with a class in a new school when they move to a new post.

Initial Teacher Education programmes rely heavily on experienced teachers (mentors) having the necessary skills to be able to transfer their tacit knowledge ('ie what works in this school context') to trainee teachers, but as this knowledge is inextricably bound up with their personal experience, and given the fact that there are significant differences of context, students, school values and structures, the efficacy of this as a model for the dissemination of research and investigation outcomes is questionable. This can lead to a lack of purposeful engagement and a tangible disillusionment with educational research, especially as the research teaching for trainees at the university often carries concomitant assessment requirements that trainees may have little hope of fulfilling. Contrary to this pessimistic outlook as described by Hargreaves (1999), in 2018 there are a growing number of forms of dissemination, as witnessed by Poultney (2017) when working in partnership to support evidence-based teaching approaches in a primary school. Active leadership support helped to provide teachers in the school with 'safe spaces' in which to discuss their research and to display their outcomes around the school. In this case, the research work undertaken in the school resulted in the publication of a book aimed at school-based classroom practitioners.

## University partnership model

As argued elsewhere (Day, 1999; Poultney, 2017), the role of a university partner is integral to supporting inquiry endeavours in school. Engaging with a linear approach through the establishment of a trusting relationship can help promote research knowledge sharing but school structures, hierarchies and professional 'ways of being' are important factors to consider. Rather than seeing the models as separate, working alongside school leaders (who can assume the role of 'knowledge brokers') the most appropriate ways of disseminating knowledge across the school can be devised. Linear models then, should not be seen as separate. Academics do not have the right to privilege research knowledge over practice knowledge and should respect the professional spaces teachers work within (Hall, 2009). Working within school structures will sometimes pose challenges which can become barriers to building networks, especially if the sharing and disseminating of knowledge is by dint of an outsider (the academic) inhabiting the space between the school and the university (Campbell et al, 2017; Poultney, 2017). It is also important for academics to understand that teachers might have had limited engagement with academic literature and research and so support for theory and its translation into actionable practice is essential to maintaining a working relationship over time.

## Use of social media

The use of websites and social media such as Twitter, Facebook and Instagram can be a very effective means of sharing events (often in real time) and new ways of working. Social media can also be useful for observing how children are learning. Sharing knowledge is not the preserve of teachers alone, either within or across schools, and parents can have an important part to play as they support their children's learning. Poultney (2017), writing about action learning, found the use of Twitter was an effective means of communicating to parents about/concerning what children were learning. This was often achieved in real time through tweets in class, which provided a drip feed of information to parents and promoted further dialogue with parents and/or children in person.

## Use of innovation hubs

As teachers begin to gain confidence from undertaking their research work, many find that they turn more frequently to academic literature before deciding on the best course of action in school. Most Teaching School Alliances, Trusts and Multi-Academy Trusts have a designated Research and Development committee that is focused on up-to-date research and which makes these outcomes available to schools. Innovation hubs, journal clubs and similar provide a space for teachers to share their own research and to make available synopses of their own reading of research. These spaces are also where university academics can share their work and offer guidance on the setting up of research projects. Cain (2015a) found that teachers are able to transform academic research knowledge into pedagogical knowledge specifically by taking the propositional and theoretical knowledge from research and modifying it accordingly by drawing upon their own concepts developed through their teaching experiences, thus reducing the generalised cases depicted in research. This 'enlightenment' comprised conceptual development, reflection on cases drawn from personal experience and the imaginative diffusion of research knowledge into areas beyond those originally researched (Cain, 2015a, p 505). Cain's work demonstrates that in order for research to have any impact on the practice of teachers, and for knowledge to be mobilised from the academy to the school, practitioners are required to engage with research (and with university academics), so that they can feel the benefits from research first hand. For policy-makers there is no quick fix, despite enthusiasm for such initiatives such as RCTs.

## External meetings and conferences

Meetings and conferences external to school present excellent opportunities to share new knowledge. University partners routinely engage in conferences which serve both professional and academic audiences and where practitioner voice in particular is very welcomed. In their research with middle leaders, Stoll et al (2018, p 58) found that knowledge sharing opportunities are best created when:

> ...middle (teacher) leaders create a culture for learning with openness to dialogue, where people can speak their minds in a safe environment, issues are explored, and experimentation and acceptable risk taking is encouraged.

The most effective middle leaders were those who:

> ...created opportunities to share successes and innovation, using professional learning forums, meetings, newsletters, and social media

**to help build shared objectives around knowledge exchange, and were
supported by time and resources.**

(Stoll et al, 2018, p 59)

## 4.6  Teachers engaging with research

Much of the research conducted in education has little impact on classroom practice because findings created from research do not chime with the
personal practice or personal knowledge teachers deploy in the classroom.
Findings from research are presented as codified knowledge and are only
useful to teachers if the evidence can be used to overcome a problem or improve their own practice. If evidence is regarded as explicit knowledge then it
represents a view of the world that may differ from the classroom as experienced by a teacher. This is especially so when teachers work together and
bring their different perspectives about how to use research outcomes or how
to use research to generate new knowledge. Rickinson et al (2011) refer to this
as 'close to practice' research, which is closely aligned with teachers' professional values and identities.

Using research evidence in a classroom successfully is predicated on using
personal knowledge in two ways: for teaching and for reflection. A proficient
teacher's actions will be immediately observable in the classroom as will the
use of personal orientations that depend on the situation and context faced by
the teacher. Outside the classroom, a teacher may draw upon their espoused
knowledge; how they choose to describe their approaches to teaching. Teachers may draw on personal knowledge, for example, when mentoring a trainee
teacher. Trainees often trust that experienced teachers will know what to do
in certain situations but struggle to understand how to replicate the observed
practice in their own teaching. Teachers also have their own philosophy or
educational aims with regard to schooling, a form of moral compass that sets
the direction for their educational practice. Schön (1983, p 5) labels practical
modes of knowledge as 'knowing in action' and 'reflecting in action'. Knowing
in action is a way in which teachers act when their practice is not challenged;
when they do not need to solve a problem. When solving a problem is necessary, however, teachers 'reflect in action', stepping back from the situation and
restructuring their actions in the light of the changed circumstance. Teachers
therefore use their personal orientations to frame their own teaching practice.

Teaching is a complex system of ideas, habituated practice and individual
teacher values, and is shaped by external (and ever-changing) government
policy. Day to day, teachers are required to make quick decisions about how
and what knowledge they are imparting to students amid a constant stream
of information coming from school management, colleagues, media sources,

government and academic research (Hall, 2009). Much of the evidence now collected by schools for external scrutiny by the inspectorate is measurable data related to student performance and national tests that suggest minimum baseline standards for each age phase of education. This results in vast numbers/amounts of data, which becomes seductive and hard to argue against – the *'facts speak for themselves'* and *'hard evidence which is difficult to refute'* (Biesta, 2017).

If teachers are to engage with published academic research as both investigators and producers, then the research must reflect the context in which teachers are working. It might be reasonable to expect that teachers engaging in their own research projects develop a confidence to engage with academic research and begin to develop a personalised professional research vocabulary most suited to their professional context. In contrast to the medical model of research described elsewhere in this book, teachers are not seeking to discover universal laws of truth about/underlying a problem, but do want to know more about the problem itself, and how it might be manifested in different contexts. In encouraging teachers to become research-engaged as opposed to research-interested, the motivation has to be steeped in a greater pursuit of understanding of a problem, and the nature of the knowledge or *'epistemic tools'* (Hall, 2009, p 673) has to chime with the ontological perspectives of teachers' worlds. Teachers engaging, who also act as researchers, become the producers of knowledge. They critically engage with other teachers about the outcomes of their work, and become more autonomous and less accepting of the next new initiative.

Hargreaves (1999, p 128) quoting Huberman (1983) suggests that:

> ...the recipes are traded on the basis of a validity that is craft embedded and highly experiential... Research evidence is an unlikely source of practitioner information, not only because it assumes an underlying order but also because the ways in which the theoretical or scientific sources talk and write about instrumental practice are uncongenial: the two frames of reference collide.

Teachers might be better equipped to digest and use research if they have a higher degree, such as a Master's qualification, but as this is not a professional requirement and is, therefore, often an individual endeavour, the take-up is likely to remain patchy. In their systematic review of the use of research to improve professional practice, Hemsley-Brown and Sharp (2003) found two main themes: the need for cultural change and management strategies. These two areas also held true for medicine but focusing on education issues around designing research, training, forming networks, collaboration, partnerships and communication networks were integral to schools becoming research-engaged.

The use of research outcomes and knowledge mobility in the public sector is ineffective when it is related to the work of individual practitioners. The way in which social science research is constructed and presented can lead to challenge around the context, trustworthiness (validity and reliability) and transferability or generalisability of the findings. Such scrutiny can bring findings of small-scale projects into doubt and do not help to encourage practitioners to engage fully in their own research.

At the organisational level, it is the role of managers to promote and invest in research and its outcomes. Research documentation is usually housed in universities rather than schools, and this, coupled with the perception that the language of research is (often) esoteric/abstruse and unrelated to practice, means that research is often disregarded by the profession.

A more positive position regarding both access and use of research was reported by those engaged in study at Master's level, although the contrasting goals of teachers and academics remain stark. Given the practical/pragmatic nature of classroom teaching, it is not surprising to note that, when questioned, practitioners commented on the need for speedy answers to operational problems. Academics, on the other hand, remain firmly ensconced in knowledge production (Mode 1). The validity of research for practitioners, it seems, depends on whether it can be translated into practical (Mode 2) knowledge.

Engagement in Level 7 (Master's) study clearly enables teachers to develop a critical eye on matters related to education policy, but without close collaboration with managers or those in positions to effect change, the knowledge gained is destined to remain at local teacher level. With regard to issues of school improvement, engagement with research was not seen by teachers as an effective means of raising standards. This is because schools are social systems and knowledge is socially (professionally) and politically constructed as part of a hierarchical organisation which might militate against teacher involvement in change management. Empirical studies in this review indicated that practitioners need to be involved in the design, implementation and dissemination of research findings. Dissemination, however, may also be limited to local impact and the authors identified legalisation and adequate funding as the two means by which adoption of change would take place.

## Translational research

One of the persistent discourses in education centres around school improvement and improving the quality of education for all children. Over the last three decades the focus has been on raising standards. Children are routinely measured and tested, and schools are inspected against a set of quality benchmarks which are made publicly available. The one overriding factor is that the quality of our education system is inherently linked to the quality of the teachers who make up the workforce. Stenhouse's (1975) view of the classroom as a laboratory encompasses the notion of teachers reaching a consensus regarding the creation of a professional knowledge-base through development of their own theories which would be evidence-rich and available for all teachers to access and use. In reality, we have many published small-scale research projects (mainly from academia) that are not always readily available to practitioners despite the plea from the BERA-RSA Inquiry (2014, p 8) into the role of research in education:

**Producers of research knowledge, including universities, teaching school alliances, academy chains and local authorities, as well as individual schools, endeavour to make their research findings as freely available, accessible and usable as possible.**

However, whose evidence do you trust? As is often the case in schools, there are as many opinions about, for example, how to get boys reading as there are teachers discussing the problem. No one knows with certainty what will work in practice, and basing interventions work on information from rather expensive longitudinal projects undertaken by consultants is no guarantee of success.

There is no real school infrastructure that helps teachers make good research-informed decisions. Many of these decisions are heavily based on politics, traditional teaching approaches, external marketing and anecdotal information. In the absence of such educational architecture, teachers need to be personally 'research-savvy'. As producers of knowledge, they will develop confidence in the validity of their own findings and will be in a much stronger position to drive school improvement. The needs of the individual teachers in their classrooms must be recognised; teachers interact with their students throughout the day and have little time to apply research findings in the classroom. Yet there comes a point at which teachers must make decisions about 'what works', and this is where they need to trust that research outcomes can be translated into practical application in the classroom.

Jones et al (2015) suggest that drawing on the medical model 'The Map of Medicine' helps not just doctors but also patients who wish to improve the quality of health care (http://mapofmedicine.com/). They argue that online networks and communities of practice similar to the map of medicine could provide the missing link between the outcomes of research and practice, and provide a speedy solution for teachers assessing ways forward in their own practice.

This type of e-infrastructure used in health circles is now also found in local government; see the 'Knowledge Hub' https://khub.net/ (Leask, 2011).

Reducing the gap between the use of research findings and practice, and giving fast access to a variety of knowledge bases, would enable teachers to have a ready source of evidenced-based information to help in their decision-making. Through working with others, knowledge can be mobilised, exchanged and translated; and the building of social networks that encompass researchers and practitioners is much more likely to lead to the reciprocal dissemination of research outcomes that are understood and valued by both parties (Jones et al, 2015).

The Education Futures Collaboration (EFC) has, as one of its aims, developed a translational research tool called 'Mapping Educational Specialist know-How', known as the MESH guides: www.meshguides.org/mesh-guides/. This website provides access to international research, using volunteers from a number of countries to provide research summaries of their research. It encourages educators from all phases of education, including university academics, to submit guides which are blind-peer-reviewed to provide a measure of quality assurance that supports professional judgement with evidence and a means of partnership working. The website is free to use, and as Jones et al (2015, p 561) explain, the guides *aim to end the hermetically sealed circle of research being only available in academic journals, which are not accessible to teachers and are normally read almost solely by other academics*. The improvement in technology means that practitioners and researchers can collaborate to review, discuss and generate research via the internet and the online platform. These online part-nership spaces allow for feedback to the authors of the translational research guides, and the results of putting the theory into practice in the classroom and feeding back on the outcomes can reduce the divide between academia and practising teachers.

In researching how teachers used the MESH guides, Jones et al (2015) found that although teachers were positive about the site (commenting on its ease of access and use), they would not access it on a regular basis, preferring to use it to address a specific problem, or to provide some evidence for their decisions, in mentoring a student teacher or planning for INSET training. The review re-vealed the predilection of teachers to act as consumers rather than creators of research and the notion that they required permission to engage with research was prevalent.

Teachers are required to constantly recast their practice and to contribute to professional learning communities of practice so that their professional know-ledge and experiences can be shared. Jones et al (2015, p 571) conclude that:

> The challenge now is how to turn this [Web 2.0 technologies supporting the MESH guides] into a sustainable ecosystem so that practitioners can add to the development of new knowledge, thereby truly embedding translational research in the field of education.

Cordingley (2008) cautions that school leaders should restrict research outcomes to issues that are closely related to teachers' needs and their own interests. Interpretation of these and other policy issues coming into school from government will require some form of interpretation and architecture for research knowledge to be translated at the classroom level.

## 4.7  Key debates about knowledge mobilisation and implications for education

### 1. *Evidence-based approach versus a democratic, professional approach*

There is a large body of research literature, some of which favours a research-based approach to education, yet a substantial number of academics question whether it is as simple as using research evidence to raise educational standards. For authors such as Goldacre (2013) and Shavelson et al (2003), allegiance to scientific research is unswerving. This 'medical model' of research which advocates the use of RCTs (the most common method used in clinical trials) has been contested by Biesta, (2007, 2015, 2017), Slavin (2002), and Torgerson and Torgerson (2003) for being too narrow an approach. This notion is also supported by Cain (2015a). For these authors, such evidence on its own is not a sufficient outcome on which the teaching profession should be judged. Put simply, evidence in the form of 'hard measurable data' is eroding what it is to be a teacher professional. Biesta (2017) argues for the reclamation of professional democracy, where the privileging of markets, customers and standards is set against professional approaches that give meaning and a sense of direction to education. He sees democracy as a set of committed values centred on equality, liberty and solidarity. Biesta (2017) writes that teachers who recognise the importance of the continued well-being of their students, and those that see teaching as more than the collection of data on their students, seek to promote 'educatedness' – the development of cognitive and moral independence in their students (Biesta, 2017, p 325–26).

### 2. *Capacity for research*

Hemsley-Brown and Sharp (2003) and Hargreaves (1999) ask what motivators are best used to implement research – financial and legislative. They ask who should act as support for the implementation of research findings – academics, school leaders or local authorities? This is a complex, wide-ranging issue, and is about more than apportioning blame or castigating individual teachers for not engaging with research. Thinking about how to translate research findings into actionable pedagogical practice, Jones et al (2015) and Leask (2011) support the use of knowledge-management (KM) tools and Web 2.0 tools as a way of helping teachers access a wide body of educational knowledge. They also advocate the development of an e-infrastructure to support education to become a knowledge industry so that knowledge building and knowledge sharing becomes common practice within and across countries worldwide.

## 3. *Insufficient Evidence*

Leask's study in 2011 suggested there was an insufficient evidence-base coming from research into teacher education, classroom practice, subject-specific pedagogy and special educational needs (SEN). Although there was evidence of numerous small-scale studies, none were able to effect policy changes due to poor reporting of the evidence-base and the lack of means to link up researchers working on common themes. Promising small-scale research was not scaled up and reporting procedures often made outcomes inaccessible to teachers, resulting in little impact on changing practice. E-Systems can provide fast and effective low-cost opportunities for universities to engage in knowledge transfer with end-users of research, but ad hoc use of websites is not validated via citations accorded to their evidence. If policy is to be predicated on evidence, then end-users need to have access to robust, validated findings. The speed and accessibility (to teachers) of research findings emerging in e-format and print is woefully slow; and as time is needed for the peer review process and subsequent publication to take place, some findings (though intrinsically interesting) may not keep pace with educational changes. Use of synchronous and asynchronous communication can benefit the opportunities for large-scale research and the dissemination of findings to a wider audience. Leask (2011, p 650) suggests that one of the main advantages of communication through social networking-type sites is the revealing of teacher tacit knowledge or 'coffee-break conversations' that produce knowledge in the here and now, unlike CPD programmes which rely on 'yesterday's knowledge'.

## 4. *Forms of knowledge needed to undertake research*

The type of knowledge required to promote professional learning and improve practice has already been identified by Shulman (1987) and updated by Leask (2011). This wide range of knowledge, much of it complex and diverse, has to be accessed, assimilated and re-worked by teachers to meet the ever-changing landscape of education and the fast-paced nature of work in schools. Today, teachers have a wealth of ways in which to advance their knowledge following graduation:

- formal CPD routes;
- interaction with colleagues;
- higher education provider;
- school networks;
- local authorities;
- professional associations;
- print-based sources;
- inspectorate;
- government circulars/publications;
- websites and databases.

The software to mine this wealth of online information needs to be fine-grained and appropriate to meet the needs of practice. Until this is the case, some of the most effective ways that teachers can generate new research or knowledge are:

- engaging in research and development – co-construction of knowledge with other practitioners;
- engaging with CPD that meets the needs of teachers – CPD that has teachers' professionalism and individual expertise as its core value;
- ensuring CPD is personalised towards the needs of teachers at different stages of their careers;
- collaboration through professional learning communities (PLCs) (Leask, 2011; Stoll et al, 2018).

The use of such e-platforms for knowledge sharing is, in theory, a reasonable solution to the age-old problem of teacher access to up-to-date knowledge and the translation of research findings in individual schools. The establishment of e-systems requires an independent professional body to fund and oversee its initial setup and subsequent running. Giving an independent body oversight of such a system would ensure its trustworthiness and provide some assurance to the education community with regard to its independence from government. The professional credentials of the users of the websites would need to be validated in order to be accepted onto the platform.

Having access to knowledge for education professionals and being able to produce knowledge are key components of a national e-system, and the infrastructure would need financial support to ensure that knowledge is properly archived at the end of funded projects. There is still scant evidence regarding how such systems impact on student attainment or, indeed, how practitioners might be made accountable with regard to their engagement with such networks. The positives of this e-infrastructure are, to date, around attempting to join together academics, teacher educators, teachers, policy-makers and national and international initiatives (Jones et al, 2015).

Dewey (1929) saw education as a science where teachers had a vested interest in their own work and how they might operate as teacher-researchers in better understanding their own practice. Stenhouse (1975) saw the classroom as a laboratory, a place where teachers might experiment (or take risks with their pedagogy in today's parlance), to build a repository of teaching and learning knowledge. Stenhouse wanted teachers not to be mere practitioners but professionals informed by knowledge, and with a clear set of articulated values together with a repertoire of practical skills. Classroom practitioners should be central to curriculum development and research. Schön (1983) stressed the importance of reflection as an activity from which teachers can learn from their practice and build 'practice wisdom'. This, in turn, can promote engagement in professional learning and a deeper understanding of the complex relationship between pedagogical approaches and effective student learning. Experience of practice improves teacher learning and bestows the authority to teach. In beginning research on practice, teachers may draw upon a wide range of experiences, and in the fast-paced world of teaching today the many factors that interact in their classrooms may make them reluctant to focus on a seemingly narrow issue. Asking teachers to draw on research literature, however sourced, is problematic and teachers may ask the following questions:

## Questions for enquiry in your own school

- What type of literature will best inform the concern I have identified?

- How do I source this literature: online search engine, through specific Web 2.0 technologies?

- What methodologies do I use to research my concern?

- How do I develop the space to research a narrow aspect of my practice when so many new concerns seem to arrive daily?

This is possibly why teachers are so keen to embrace new pre-prepared interventions designed to effect some form of change. Sometimes these interventions will fail and may reinforce the view that researching into why it failed will in some way expose the teacher's own incompetence. Yet many of these teacher stories, if shared, would provide an evidence-base for further discussion and learning opportunities. Unlike academia, where the academic has a duty to publish the results of their research, teachers are under no such obligation. For teacher-led research to be effective, a culture of professional trust needs to be nurtured so that teachers feel free to discuss their work openly.

The following account details how a collaborative approach can be used to identify teacher concerns and to build teacher confidence around the sharing of praxis knowledge. For each of the three stages of active learning, the following case study illustrates the rationale for how the teachers approached the research, what they did and how their newly acquired pedagogical knowledge helped to raise their confidence and their willingness to share their outcomes with other teachers.

## Case study 1

Helen had some concerns about the lack of interaction between her Year 6 pupils and their very passive approach to learning. Using a superhero theme for learning such as Mr Resourceful, Mr Resilient and so on, Helen adopted a more child-centred approach to learning based on the school's Foundation Stage ways of learning. In endeavouring to get the children to engage more interactively with their learning and to promote more independent learning, Helen researched a pedagogical style based on the work of Ryan and Gilbert (2011) called active learning, which challenges children's thinking using real-life and imaginary activities. The active element of the lesson involved more group working, outdoor learning and competitive-type activities, all of which was a different pedagogical approach from the more formal learning style of the Year 6 classroom. Working with Laura, her partner Year 6 teacher and NQT, both teachers developed a new pedagogical approach where the learner was placed at the centre of the classroom, not the teacher. Helen and Laura talked to other staff about their work informally, showed them videos of their active learning lessons, and using time in a series of staff meetings used the pedagogy of active learning to engage the staff in discussions about questioning, marking and assessment. Some staff felt confident to develop their own active learning sessions, after observing Year 6 active learning sessions.

### Stage 1: Collaboration with others

Identify an issue with teaching or learning or both. Focus on the issue, do not make it personal. Make sure you are dealing with the bigger picture. Who else has identified a similar issue? Move beyond the classroom context (treat it as context, not as the reason for the concern) and involve the views of other teachers to reframe the issue under investigation. As a group, you are less exposed and can focus on the problem, from which your own professional learning may be consolidated.

Helen and Laura were concerned about collecting evidence for active learning but they asked the children to focus on what they had learnt and whether they had enjoyed their learning while becoming more responsible for their own learning. They took photographs of the lessons, recorded videos using 'Class Watch' (a 360-degree working video) and engaged other staff in active learning pedagogies. They both began to develop a growing confidence in this new approach to learning, and their classrooms became places where other teachers could observe and share their research. Both Year 6 teachers took the opportunity to share their work within school and in CPD sessions, and the sharing of this new knowledge contributed to a shared increase in confidence for both of them.

### Stage 2: Develop your confidence

Teachers develop a sense of self-confidence as they experience 'successful' outcomes in their work, comprising a list of criteria around 'what works' for them. Sometimes, when undertaking any form of research, these underlying 'truths' may be questioned. This instils a sense of vulnerability and teacher-researchers need to learn there will be periods of personal conflict and a sense of dissonance. The school structures that support research must recognise that there will be successes and failures with research and appreciate that every engagement with research is a learning opportunity.

**Case study 3**

Helen and Laura found that some teachers were very sceptical about active learning and not all teachers were convinced it was appropriate for their classrooms. Some resented being asked to act themselves as learners as Helen and Laura disseminated their work at a staff meeting. However, despite such reservations, Helen and Laura felt they had, through some basic research into action learning, found a different pedagogical approach that was worth exploring in more depth. By piloting the approach and experiencing positive learning outcomes from the children and the teachers, they as professionals become more confident about their work and more secure that this new knowledge would have significant benefits for Year 6 children and possibly other year groups also. Communicating their research with other teachers allowed them to reflect on their own work and engage in further dialogue about active learning, despite some negative responses.

### Stage 3: Find your audience

Dissemination of your findings is a key activity so that your narrative will be heard by a wider audience of teachers in your school. As many teachers struggle with similar issues related to teaching and learning, they should be a receptive audience; however, you need to find a form of dialogue that will resonate with your teacher audience and be prepared to be challenged by their questions. This activity provides another learning opportunity for you, and your confidence will grow each time you communicate your ideas either through live presentation or in writing. Don't be afraid to discuss activities that were not as successful as everyone can learn from these 'mistakes'. It is likely that every teacher will have experienced similar events in their teaching career, so including these is a good 'leveller'. Helen was persuaded that her active learning approach would be a good example for a chapter in a book about evidence-based teaching (Poultney, 2017). The published chapter immortalised their work and added credibility in a way that teachers rarely experience.

## 4.8  Summary

Challengers of the 'gold standard' of RCTs and evidence-based only approaches to education have made clear that ignoring teachers' professional judgements is a threat to their professional democracy and a way of stifling their ability to generate specific knowledge for teaching. Many argue that teachers, like academics, generate a form of codified knowledge that could be used to re-conceptualise propositional (theoretical) forms of knowledge and provide an evidence-base for different forms of teacher knowledge. Teachers need to engage with and in research and develop the skills to translate propositional knowledge for use in their own practice. Web 2.0 technologies have provided teachers with access to a range of research summaries specifically focused on their work. The challenge remains as to how to encourage teachers to become more involved in educational research and how they may begin to collaborate with policy-makers, academics and other stakeholders so that practice wisdom can be shared.

The creating, sharing and translating of educational knowledge can be a challenge to both academic and professional communities. The dissonance between traditional peer-reviewed academic research (Mode 1 propositional knowledge) is quite different from pedagogical research (Mode 2 knowledge) which supports swift and fluent thinking. Researching practitioners produce a form of knowledge which is context-bound, specific to practice and rarely peer-reviewed for validation of truths. Academic knowledge, on the other hand, is more generalisable in its outcomes, reviewed within the academic community and held up as the 'gold standard' methodologically.

The mark of a good quality education system today is predicated predominately on outcomes which showcase metrics as opposed to other ways of making judgements about quality. Teachers, through their professional training, amass different forms of knowledge about their own subject, pedagogical approaches, classrooms, schools and the position of education in society. Like academic knowledge, it is propositional; a form of codified knowledge which forms the school's intellectual capital. School improvement discourses draw upon this capacity and enable schools to use this knowledge to make informed decisions about how to educate their students. Teachers engaged in research, either as part of an accredited course or through teacher inquiry, are better placed to conceptualise and discuss practice more critically than those teachers who are not. Teachers who operate as consumers of knowledge only, fail to provide an evidence-base for the judgements and choices they make about their practice.

Academics are often accused of not doing enough to translate knowledge from traditional research to actionable knowledge in schools. School leaders have a responsibility to establish the culture and architecture for staff to engage in research and to consider which leadership roles are most influential in this regard (Brown and Zhang, 2016). Academics can help to address some of the challenges around teachers' lack of access to university resources such as library databases and can work as knowledge brokers to support teachers engaging with their own research or interpreting that of others.

Engagements with web-based free repositories which provide summaries of research are an easy and accessible route to different forms of knowledge for teachers; the databases receive contributions from both academics and practitioners and in some cases are peer-reviewed. The value of teacher engaging/engagement in the production of research knowledge has been recognised over many decades. Very recently the BERA-RSA (2014) report provided evidence to attest to this view. Yet the fact remains that the infrastructure for this work remains weak and there is no obligation for teachers to engage in research. Teachers' standards, the inspection framework and the fragmented school landscape would appear to militate against a common framework that would permit a healthier way to promote knowledge mobilisation. Until we see more drastic measures through the standards and inspection framework that require teachers and teacher educators to take responsibility for promoting research, then it is unlikely that the inertia currently experienced by nascent teacher-researchers in schools will remain/be addressed.

These websites are a good place to begin searching for some close to practice research information. While you may be very familiar with the EEF website, it is often worth exploring a few websites to be able to gain a wider understanding of different research approaches.

Centre for Evaluating and Monitoring (CEM): www.cem.org/evidence-based-education

Coalition for Evidence-based Education (CEBE): www.cebenetwork.org

Education Endowment Fund (EEF): https://educationendowmentfoundation.org.uk/our-work/resources-centre/research-use-survey

MESH guides: www.meshguides.org/

ResearchEd: https://researched.org.uk/

Teacher Development Trust: http://tdtrust.org/

The Research-Informed Practice Site (TRIPS): www.curee.co.uk/our-projects/research-informed-practice-site-trips

What Works Network: www.gov.uk/what-works-network

York University Best Evidence in Brief: www.york.ac.uk/iee/news/beib

# Chapter 5
# **Professional learning communities and Rounds**

## 5.1  Chapter overview

This chapter will outline:

5.2   an introduction to and key ideas about professional learning communities (PLCs);

5.3   dialogic enquiry;

5.4   Learning Rounds;

5.5   case studies of PLCs.

## 5.2  Introduction and key ideas

One of the current trends in educational improvement today is around the use of 'big data' or large-scale data such as the PISA (Programme for International Student Assessment) scores which have re-cast education policy internationally in both positive and negative ways. PISA is, and remains, an influential indicator of educational standards internationally (Harris et al, 2018). Contemporary education reform privileges a business model where there is competition between teachers and schools, accountability through test scores and inspectorate outcomes, and an increasing move towards private providers of education. Some educationalists see this as an erosion of public schooling and a deprofessionalisation of educators (National Education Union, 2018). In stark contrast, there is another view of education reform that focuses upon extending professional agency and involvement of teachers as the main point of leverage in effecting educational change. In Finland, for example, a more collaborative approach focusing on professional engagement of teachers is seen as a better way to secure school improvement. The Finnish government invests 30 times more in the professional development of its teachers than it does in testing its students (Sahlberg, 2012). In terms of evidence, there is an array of academics who can attest to the ways in which professional development through investment in teachers has helped to improve schools (Watson, 2014; Day, 2017; Jones, 2017; Voelkel and Chrispeels, 2017; Harris et al, 2018).

## Understanding a professional learning community

A literature search for the phrase 'professional learning community' will reveal many sources related to the idea of teachers working together to solve problems through undertaking knowledge creation. As a social exercise, engaging in any form of professional learning, whether together or alone, can be beneficial for all participants. Hargreaves and Fullan (2012) see this work as a form of 'social capital'. Day (2017) refers to this as the establishment of 'human capital', which is likely to engender trust and a sense of individual and collective well-being which will motivate teachers to engage in activities directly related to raising school standards. Stoll et al (2006) draw on a range of international evidence in their extensive review of the PLC literature which suggests that both individually and collectively teachers can build capital that has a positive impact on students' learning. This research, funded by the DfE and NCSL, was the first of its type in the UK and it examines five broad questions which are briefly addressed in Table 5a.

**Table 5a A summary of questions and responses you might ask about PLCs (drawn from Stoll et al, 2006)**

| Questions about PLCs | Responses to questions about PLCs |
|---|---|
| What are professional learning communities? | A group of professionals who, working as a collective enterprise, seek to learn, share, reflect, enhance and improve their practice to the benefit of their students. |
| What makes professional learning communities effective? | Working towards mutual trust, respect and support that is focused on sharing professional ideals, a sense of purpose and a willingness to take on responsibility to work as part of the PLC and to be judged by other members as doing so. Engaging in reflective dialogue focused on the generation and application of new knowledge gained through meaningful inquiry but also understanding there may be conflict through normal organisational micropolitics and acknowledging that disagreements and difference are all part of a normal improvement process. |

| | |
|---|---|
| What processes are used to create and develop an effective professional learning community? | Finding ways to build expert knowledge that underpins the professional element of all teachers' work. For knowledge to be mobilised, teachers require opportunities to learn through work-based and academic routes that help to promote inquiry and better use of school data/evidence. Engaging in serious dialogue that is based on meaningful evidence, that does not privilege one voice over another, and is carried out with integrity will help to mobilise new knowledge and prolong the improvement process. |
| What other factors help or hinder the creation and development of effective professional learning communities? | The success of the PLC is dependent upon the school leaders and their ability to drive, establish and maintain the conditions necessary for teachers to learn (OECD, 2016). It has been shown that where school leaders adopt an inquiry focus and where they act as role models (with a focus on student and teacher learning through the judicious use of evidence), PLCs are much more likely to succeed. Investing in teachers through sound emotional leadership and taking steps to raise teacher morale supports the creation of PLCs. Managing resources such as time allocation, space and opportunities for the PLC to meet, work and disseminate their practice, and use of partners and internal and external networks have been found to be good support. On the negative side, PLC dynamics can be affected by school size, its history, teacher mobility, challenging local communities, school phase, teacher motivation and the structures available to provide good quality teacher development opportunities. |
| Are effective professional learning communities sustainable? | In the longer term perhaps not as the goals of the PLC are realised, but the value of this model of teacher learning can be used to address other areas of internal/external change. An evaluation of the effectiveness of the PLC and better understanding of its use would be a strong strategic model. |

## 5.3  Dialogic enquiry

PLCs have been imagined as *'a group of people sharing and critically interrogating their practice in an ongoing, reflective, collaborative, inclusive, learning orientated, growth-promoting way'* (Watson, 2014, p 19). These positive overtones have been echoed recently elsewhere in the literature (Day, 2017; Harris et al, 2018) yet it is important to understand that PLCs do not just 'come together' and return successful outcomes without sustained investment from school leadership and the development of a set of protocols for how they will operate. Table 5a provides some basic information about how school leaders can provide the architecture for the creation of PLCs. The range of types of PLCs is very broad and includes communities drawn from teaching and support staff, parents, university academics, and other educational stakeholders. The composition of PLCs is for the school(s) to agree and will, therefore, vary between establishments. The role of the PLC will also vary depending upon the task it is set. There is, however, one common component that underpins successful PLCs: dialogue.

The success or failure of a PLC rests on the quality of the participants' dialogue and the extent to which the community understands and invests in protocols for how these dialogues will be conducted. Holmlund Nelson et al (2010) noted that the quality of teachers' conversations in a PLC could limit the outcomes, and illustrated this with real-life examples of two types of conversations teachers might use in group situations: the 'congenial conversation' and the 'deep conversation' or 'collegial dialogue'. The congenial conversation is one that is polite and superficial, normally focused on narratives of practice, possibly akin to the informal stories told by teachers in staffrooms at break and lunchtimes. The deep or collegial dialogue necessary to 'bottom out' problematic areas of practice is rather more challenging because it relies on teachers using evidence such as research or student data to probe more deeply into the issue. Drawing on Himley (1991, p 59), Holmlund Nelson et al try to better understand how, over time and in a PLC context, teachers are able to move away from superficial narratives to dialogue that generates meaning and knowledge:

**Essentially this kind of talk asks participants to engage in a process of collaboratively generated meaning that takes place over a relatively long period of time... This reflective or descriptive process enables participants to see and re-see that shared focus of interest in view of an ever-enlarging web of comments, tensions, connections, connotations, differences, oppositions.**

In challenging schools, or where schools simply focus on maintaining the status quo, teachers might use sharing conversations to defend their private space (the classroom) and to better understand how effective their colleagues are as teachers. This means that deeper fault lines relating to issues of teaching and learning can be avoided, even when they are evident through classroom observations.

In an effective PLC teachers will encounter conflict, and the key here is to de-personalise the issue and to regard such conflict as an intellectual challenge. School leaders are probably in the best place to help move teachers on from congenial to collegial conversations by role modelling a more objective stance based on questioning – moving towards an evidence-based, non-judgemental dialogue that leads to discussion and action. There may be some cognitive conflict at this point as teachers might not agree at first on what approach to take, but consensus regarding the main issue under question is more likely to result from collegial rather than congenial conversations. In reality, as the case studies in this chapter demonstrate, teachers are normally grateful for the opportunity to engage in 'honest talk' in a safe environment which may well be outside of the school itself.

Holmlund Nelson et al (2010, p 178) suggest the following protocols to move away from congenial conversations:

1. Asking and answering probing questions about the reasons for, impacts of, and evidence that supports implementing specific instructional decisions.

2. Recognising the value of cognitive conflict as a way to gain a deeper understanding about the complexities of teaching and learning.

3. Being intentional about and accountable for the nature of the dialogue in collaborative group work.

4. Accessing and using tools (eg protocols and question prompts) to support a shift from congenial to collegial conversations.

The term 'professional learning community' (PLC) is, in and of itself, contested; and there are some academics who clearly wish to see a re-examination of it. Watson (2014), in examining the assumptions underpinning the PLC as a vehicle for teacher learning and change, argues that teachers and some academics have become complacent in describing its role. Drawing on the work of Louise Stoll et al (2006, p 229), Watson (2014, p 19) sees the PLC as *a group of people sharing and critically interrogating their practice in an ongoing, reflective, collaborative, inclusive, learning orientated, growth-promoting way'*. These positive overtones are echoed elsewhere in the literature (Day, 2017; Harris et al, 2018), yet it is important to understand that to evidence these behaviours in school takes considerable investment. Not all teachers are motivated to engage in a

PLC, and it is not the case that all school leaders are prepared to adequately resource PLCs to ensure their proper functioning.

Bottery (2003) makes a case for school leaders to invest in PLCs, in the spirit of re-energising the teaching profession which is currently predicated on a performative culture. There will always be some obstacles to creating and sustaining PLCs. Many teachers are not motivated enough to engage with career-long learning and some may actively subvert PLCs through setting up informal micropolitical groups. Others might avoid engaging with critical dialogue because they fear this will disrupt harmonious relationships with their colleagues (Bowe and Gore, 2017). Watson (2014) argues that teachers might be limited in their learning opportunities due to schools being charged with seeking continuous improvement in their practice, evidenced through pupil learning and an increase in standards. She sees this constant quest as:

**a slogan whose simplistic impossibility would render it [continuous school improvement] risible had it not been spoken seriously by so many otherwise rational professionals – may impose a narrowly instrumental or technicist agenda focused on pupil attainment as the legitimate aim of the PLC which suppresses the search for diversity, creativity and adaptability, thereby reducing its effectiveness.**

(Watson, 2014, p 27)

The enculturation of teachers using a PLC model is often mandated through the apparent sharing of vision and values. Joyce (2004) notes that it may be mainly politicians and management who use the PLC model to drive specific changes in education that are neither shared with nor instigated by teachers themselves. Examples of PLCs in the literature suggest a 'top-down model', where school leaders are charged in developing the capacity of teachers to work collaboratively (Philpott and Oates, 2017b). This point is echoed by Servage (2008, 2009); Bottery (2003) and Codd (2005), who argue that what teachers learn may be driven by government agendas so that although PLCs may on the face of it exhibit professional autonomy they are, in reality, learning content that has already been pre-determined.

Along the same lines, Pedder and Opfer (2011), in their State of the Nation study into the continuing professional development of teachers, found that teachers had limited access to learning opportunities and that they may be further disadvantaged through their own school context which might not support or make available a range of CPD opportunities related to their professional learning requirements. In more recent times, and especially where schools face challenging circumstances, the rise of Academy Trusts, Teaching School Alliances and School-University partnerships have afforded teachers the opportunity to engage in activities more suited to career-phase and individual learning needs through networked events led and managed by such providers. These types of PLCs may have the power to improve teacher agency through increased opportunities for teacher learning. There is, however, little empirical evidence of either the type of learning teachers engage with as part of a PLC or of teacher agency in action. Studies conducted by Philpott and Oates (2017a, b) used the concept of Learning Rounds to understand these two issues. The key features of PLCs and Rounds are broadly similar and are summarised in Table 5b (drawn from Philpott and Oates 2017b, pp 210-11):

**Table 5b Key features of professional learning communities and rounds**

| Professional learning communities | Rounds |
|---|---|
| Focus on student learning, not teaching | Focus on student learning, not teaching |
| Culture of collaboration where teachers work together to improve their classroom practice | Promotion of systematic collaboration between teachers |
| Promotes group and individual teacher learning | Concerned with group or systematic learning, not just individual teacher learning |
| Shared values and vision where all have collective responsibility to undertake reflective professional inquiry | Promote shared culture and knowledge |
| Focus on results through analysis of student performance data | Concerned about generation and analysis of data related to learning |

The next section explores what Learning Rounds are and how they can be used as examples of PLCs 'in action'.

## 5.4  Learning Rounds

Learning Rounds are a form of professional development based on Instructional Rounds practice developed in the USA. Rounds are also known as Teacher Rounds or Education Rounds. The term originates from a clinical approach to learning used to educate junior doctors, where a clinical consultant provides high quality training and learning opportunities for the medics. Today, this image of junior doctors hanging onto the coat tails of the expert consultant has shifted somewhat to a quality assurance approach based on documentation, communication and effective involvement of the patient in their care. As with teaching, more modern approaches to the clinical ward round now focus on moving the novice (junior) doctor through a series of cognitive steps from gathering facts and knowledge about medical practice to applying what has been learnt through demonstration in practice sessions. This moves the practitioner from theory to practice, thereby improving their professional authenticity so they become expert doctors (Reece and Klaber, 2012) and makes transparent the diagnosis and treatment to other learners.

In education, the aim of Rounds is to enable teachers to engage in critical dialogue about learning and to support their mutual learning as a group, perhaps as part of a PLC or a collaborative group of educators. Rounds as a learning concept dovetails with other approaches to teacher learning, namely that of lesson study, action research and teacher inquiry. As an approach to teacher learning, it has gained in popularity across the Americas, Europe and Asia and, in the same way as medicine uses the hospital ward as the learning context, education uses the school classroom to make student learning more transparent and understandable for all. There are two specific Rounds models: 'Teacher Rounds' based on the work of Del Prete (2013) and 'Instructional Rounds' (City et al, 2009; Philpott and Oates, 2015, 2017a, b). The difference between these two models is that the City model was originally designed to provide an evidence-base to schools about a specific school improvement issue. Problematic issues were identified and used to frame classroom observations of about 15–20 minutes. Classroom teachers are not, however, usually engaged in their learning. The Del Prete model, on the other hand, is more aligned to the medical practice of ward rounds, where trainee teachers are engaged in a learning Round hosted by experienced teachers. This approach focuses on an issue of practice ('practice-centred inquiry') with trainee learning ('learning-centred inquiry') as its central remit. In this model, the experienced teacher is required to explain the context for the students' learning and curriculum to the trainees, and will then outline the focus of their inquiry and discuss how they might engage with students during the lesson.

Post-round, the task of the trainees is to engage in reflective dialogue about their own learning and that of the students. This model is useful for knowledge mobilisation and can be transferrable to other classrooms and schools (Goodwin et al, 2015). Both approaches seek to gain evidence about how teachers might develop their own professional agencies through a community of learners who focus on a particular pedagogical issue and which is not judgemental about teacher performance. In both cases, those engaged in the observation process will learn something from the Rounds, but this might not be the teacher leading the lesson under observation.

## What do teachers do when they engage with Rounds?

Rounds are about understanding what happens in classrooms and how school systems support classroom practices that promote high quality student learning (City et al, 2009; Teitel, 2009). Normally, a group of educators will form a network comprising teachers, middle, senior leaders, external consultants, university tutors as appropriate to the problem of practice under investigation, and use a series of questions to determine reasons for underachievement, for example, or other specific issues. Over time, this network builds into a PLC where an intimate understanding of the issue can be discussed using a shared language. While it is important for the head/principal and senior leadership to be supportive of this improvement process, the problem of practice should not always be something decided by the headteacher; it should be an agreed focus of inquiry across a department, or phase of education. Table 5c below compares instructional rounds with observations for teacher performance (City et al, 2009, p 39):

**Table 5c Instructional Rounds compared with observations for teacher performance**

|  | Instructional Rounds | Evaluation of teacher performance |
|---|---|---|
| Learning stance | Inquiry: Genuinely want to learn something ourselves.<br>Main learners: the observers | Informative: Genuinely want someone else to learn something.<br>Main learner: The observed |
| Unit of improvement | Intended to improve the collective (school, system) | Intended to improve the individual |
| Accountability | Lateral (peer to peer) | Positional (top-down) |
| Output | Next level of work, collective commitments | Evaluative feedback, prescriptions for next steps |
| Primary focus in the classroom | The instructional core, especially the students and the tasks they are engaged in | The teacher |

The classroom observations are undertaken by (normally) no more than three to four people, visiting classrooms for 20–25 minutes and with a focus on the particular problem of practice. This might relate to any aspect of their learning, including student behaviour. There is no rubric for the observation; descriptive data is detailed as it is observed in an attempt to discover why a problem exists and to look for ways to resolve it. Individual observers do not share information until they have completed their task and have met for a debrief where a specific protocol is followed in order to minimise the number of judgemental decisions.

The following steps are undertaken.

1. Evidence which is specific, descriptive and related to the problem of practice is shared. This must be presented as evidence only and not related to observer judgements. The evidence might be written misconceptions noted in students' work, for example, not judgements made about the lack of objectives shared with the students.

2. Using the accumulated evidence, the group looks for patterns within it. These patterns may, for example, be particular to specific parts of the curriculum; or concern issues attributable to early career teachers. Data which does not seem to fit is noted as exceptional.

3. The protocol then requires observers to put themselves in the students' position and to ask what they would have *actually* learnt. This allows observers to be able to predict what the students might have learnt if they had had more information on a specific topic, or instruction on how to source it.

Analysing evidence in this way should help the group to both determine whether the problem of practice is real or imagined and to agree what the next steps might be. At this point it should shine a light into a dark corner of practice, which might reveal problems with assessment across the whole school. Leaders may need to provide more resources to ensure that planned changes can be actioned.

Rounds challenge adult learning (City et al, 2009) and inform the next steps in teacher development and professional learning. They become a cyclical process whereby the school action/development plan can be populated with evidence that drives future choices about teaching and learning. How often Rounds should be conducted is a choice for the school leadership but they should not be seen as one-off events. Rounds can bring a focus for inquiry into sharp relief and, as part of a PLC, teachers can gather evidence in real time and be part of a solution-focused analytical process. This data helps to build a rich learning environment for students and teachers and can be used to guide professional development so that it is specific to school and individual learning needs.

While the use of Rounds is gaining in popularity, there is very little theoretical analysis or empirical data to support this approach. There has been a positive rhetoric within the literature regarding the purpose, process, conduct and benefits of Rounds (City et al, 2009. 2011; Teitel, 2009; Goodwin et al, 2015; Philpott and Oates, 2015; Bowe and Gore, 2017; Philpott, 2017), yet a lack of theory and application to practice in support of teacher educators in their engagement with Rounds as a professional learning tool has also been acknowledged by the same group of academics.

More recently, Rounds as a research approach has been advocated by Philpott and Oates (2017a, 2017b) and Bowe and Gore (2017). However, in order to understand better how teachers learn when they are part of a PLC, we also need to understand teacher agency. Philpott and Oates (2017a, p 319) see this as interplay between teachers' past experiences and understanding and their ways of thinking and acting in any social context (iterational); the ability to envision possible future alternative ways of thinking and acting and what they are (projective); and the capacity and resources for the current situation (practical-evaluative). Previous understandings and actions can, therefore, determine future ways of thinking, understanding and subsequent acting. This might allow teachers to remain unchanged in their thinking and/or actions or give them possibilities to think and act in new ways.

While all of these elements of agency can be achieved individually or collectively, their influence on the agency of teachers remains in question. Some argue that teachers are more likely to develop their learning/agency when the appropriate structures or architecture are in place. Others argue that the development of teacher agency depends upon the ability of teachers to work with the resources and structures already available. From an initial teacher (trainee/training) perspective, Roegman and Riehl (2012, 2015) have identified similarities between the medical and educational training communities citing, among other findings, issues around power and status (leadership), concerns regarding the purpose of undertaking Rounds to develop shared norms and understanding about teaching and learning, and challenges in agreeing pedagogical approaches and subject content.

Interest in the growth of teacher agency and how this might influence the capacity for change as part of school improvement has come not only from academics but also from a reform perspective (Stoll et al, 2006; Sahlberg, 2012). PLCs have been seen as a medium through which teachers can develop their agency, both in terms of their own personal learning and as a way of either responding to, or driving, reform. Philpott and Oates (2017a, p 320) argue there is a conundrum here:

**are professional learning communities an affordance for agency or is the exercise of teacher agency a pre-requisite for professional learning communities?**

Bowe and Gore (2017) argue that the conceptualisation of professional development is, in itself, problematic. In contrast to Philpott and Oates (2017a), they acknowledge the necessity for structural resources and the need for more openness and trust among teachers as constraints to professional development. They further argue that, in its current guise, professional development makes insufficient measurable impact on practice and offer four reasons why this might be so:

1. Having respect for teachers' judgements in how they might collaborate, acknowledging the 'situatedness' of teachers' knowledge and the lack of agreement about what constitutes an effective knowledge-base for teaching.

2. Figuring out what makes good teaching is itself a wicked issue given it is an extremely complex activity.

3. Getting teachers to agree on how to collaborate (for example in a PLC) is a challenge given their diverse range of beliefs and values; relationships become fraught and strained, and agreement may be feigned.

4. Reaching agreement may be impeded by an undeveloped language teachers have for talking about their work.

(based on Bowe and Gore, 2017, p 353)

The aim of Rounds is to produce, as part of a general school improvement agenda, changes in culture which will ultimately lead to higher standards. Learning Rounds, Instructional Rounds and Educational Rounds have been used in different contexts in an attempt to understand, in a fine-grained way, 'problems of practice'. The solutions need to embrace the following components:

- a focus on the instructional core (teacher and student in the presence of content);

- evidence drawn from classroom observations;

- evidence that can be acted upon – improvement can be evidenced in real time;

- connected with a broader strategy for improvement;

- would make a significant difference to student learning.

(drawn from City et al, 2009, p 102)

The instructional core is an *'attempt to build an evidenced-informed pedagogical profile of the school'* (Bowe and Gore, 2017, p 355). There are a series of steps that allow for evaluation of the interplay between students, teacher and content. The first is based around lesson observation, which is intimately linked to the debrief step. The debriefing step is divided into four stages, which should appear in a particular order:

1. description;

2. analysis;

3. prediction;

4. evaluation.

The teachers participating in Rounds are encouraged to keep their views as non-judgemental as possible and are required to record only what they see as evidence as opposed to what they think they should see (which suggests an element of teacher bias). For instructional rounds there is a debrief protocol with questions that allow participants to share their views based on the evidence they have collected. Therefore, the more 'fine-grained' the descriptions of the observations, the more useful it will be to the group (Bowe and Gore, 2017; Philpott and Oates, 2017a). However, as Bowe and Gore make clear, asking teachers to provide an evidence-base without some form of judgement being passed is particularly tricky in the descriptive mode, and without some form of agreed consensus over what constitutes good teaching, it makes these actions challenging.

In their research focusing on four Scottish schools, Philpott and Oates (2015, 2017a) state that the outcomes of Learning Rounds were fraught with difficulties for the following reasons:

- A focus on teacher actions rather than a connection between teacher actions and student learning.

- The observers did not report evidence with a fine-grained focus on specifics of individual actions.

- Classroom activity was recorded more as an audit and good practice observed was not described in terms of how it had a positive effect.

- No theory of action proposed (link between observation data and what is/ what is not working in classrooms).

- Premature evaluations on the basis of unclear evidence.

In their research report, Philpott and Oates suggest that the teachers involved did not appreciate how to collect and use good evidence, and that they tended to *'pull to the black hole'* of existing education practice and the orthodoxy of what counts as good practice (Philpott and Oates, 2015, p 34). Consequently, they were not able to develop a theory of action. This may have been due to a lack of training for teachers on what Learning Rounds are, including their purpose and function.

As Learning Rounds do not require the intervention of an external consultant, and given that teachers do not need access to supporting academic literature, they can seem to offer a financially attractive approach to professional development for classroom practitioners in schools. Philpott and Oates note, however, that a lack of investment in the level of preparation needed to undertake Learning Rounds may have contributed to the participating schools failing to maximise the potential of the strategy as a school improvement/ teacher learning initiative/opportunity.

In the case studies below, the work of a 'knowledgeable other' or 'critical friend' as a valuable contributor to question and guide teachers working as part of a PLC is described.

## 5.5  Case studies of PLCs

Val is a great supporter of school-university partnerships as she believes teachers need space and time to think more deeply about their practice. In working with primary schools more generally around issues related to inquiry practice, it became increasingly clear that questions around leadership were beginning to dominate teacher dialogue Here, three examples are presented which illustrate how PLCs might emerge.

### Case study 1

In the first example, a group of primary middle leaders came to the university to discuss how they might adopt a more informed inquiry stance in their school planning. During the discussion it became apparent that the group were struggling with relational leadership issues, in part due to their inexperience as middle leaders and because they had all come previously from schools judged to be outstanding to this new school ranked only as good. It became clear that this group were not yet ready to take on inquiry as relational problems with longstanding, experienced primary teachers seemingly resistant to any form of change needed to be resolved. With a focus on making middle leadership more effective in this specific school context, they agreed with Val to make regular journeys to the university where they could talk freely and in depth about the barriers they were facing as a leadership group. Over the course of the next few meetings, they were able to explore some of the problems through mini case studies or 'vignettes'. Using some of the theory of emotional intelligence and leadership, the leaders tested some practical strategies for building good working relationships with class teachers.

Operating in a safe space (the university) allowed members of the middle-leader PLC to engage in critical discussion and debate without fear of judgement. Through continuing to work in this way, the leaders are building trust and beginning to understand what is possible in terms of changing teachers' hearts and minds. In addition, they are coming to a better understanding of their own role as teacher-leaders and are generating leadership knowledge which is contributing to their own learning.

## Case study 2

In the second example, two secondary school departments engaged with lesson study as part of the Research and Development strand of a Teaching School Alliance. The history department had a focus on improving General Certificate of Secondary Education (GCSE) grades and introduced lesson study to Year 10. The English department had a focus on the perceived under-performance in literacy of Year 7 students and also used lesson study as a means of generating research data. Two university partners were engaged in supporting these departments and followed up the work by interviewing these teachers, to better understand what they learnt as they engaged with lesson study and the benefits of evidence-based practice development. The teachers across the two departments reported that their learning had had impact not only within the subject departments, but across the school more widely. In addition, the teaching teams had helped to affirm positive professional relationships evidenced through a mutual trust and understanding of ways of working. The teams were moving towards a community of practice, and their shared learning through teacher inquiry had encouraged them to continue working in this way, despite some substantial challenges to resourcing and a lack of support from the wider school leadership. Organisational and structural school processes limited the opportunities for teacher inquiry to take place more widely across the school, but the benefits of teaching teams working in this way using lesson study were both beneficial for students and the staff.

## Case study 3

A federation of primary heads had been looking at ways of embedding inquiry into their primary schools as a means of improving teaching and learning.

There were three primary heads and one over-arching executive head, and it was clear from the outset that they all worked well together, but equally clear that they looked to the executive head for guidance and final decisions on matters. Only one of the schools had been judged by Ofsted as 'good'; the other two were working towards this grade for their next inspection. Again, the meetings took place at the university and it became clear that the executive head needed to step back and allow the other heads to present their points of view. All the heads recognised the opportunities and limitations of working in a federation related to equity issues: not privileging one school over another, having equality of opportunity to undertake professional development, and school micropolitics. Val suggested that their collective recent engagement with lesson study could be used as a vehicle for active engagement with inquiry and that this would provide a focus on pupil learning. In this case, the PLC agreed that staff from all three primary schools should be offered the opportunity to take part in a professional development session at the university where Val would present the theory about lesson study. It was also agreed that each school head would then make it possible (structurally) to translate this theory into practice at school in such a way that all staff could receive knowledge about lesson study and the three schools could plan to become part of a larger, networked PLC.

## 5.6  Summary

Much has been written in the academic and professional literature about the value of PLCs. They are billed as opportunities where all the positives of collaborative working suddenly materialise: trust, reciprocity, agreements and so forth. They are based on teachers learning from social interaction opportunities with their peers as compared with a transmission-type model evidenced in more traditional professional development courses. Much of this learning is also about understanding how to behave, in a community of practice, the results of which may manifest in a change of teacher identity (Lave, 1991). In reality, and acknowledging that these behaviours might prevail, there is another, less acknowledged side to PLCs which suggests they might not be quite as comfortable as initially described. PLCs and Rounds are approaches designed to raise standards and engage with school improvement issues. Unlike PLCs, Rounds discourage teachers looking at teacher performance but focus on the learning of the pupils/students. By collecting a raft of lesson evidence as a group, teachers focus on what they actually observed in the classroom and engage in critical discussion as a result. Teachers are then able to agree and share some theories about teaching and learning, which in turn helps to improve a school's intellectual and professional capacity.

Think of an example of a PLC in your school, or when a group of teachers have come together in a group – for example, a 'working group'. Make a note of the composition of the group: number of people, their role in school (class teacher, middle/senior leader, and support staff) and the purpose of setting up the group (focus on student learning, wider school issue causing concern). If you were part of such a group you should be able to answer the following:

- What was the purpose or focus of setting up the group/community?
- Who determined the composition of the group and why?
- Did the roles of each member equally contribute to the purpose of the group?
- In what ways were the group collegiate? Think of at least 2–3 examples.
- In what ways were the outcomes of the work of this group/community successful/not successful? List 2–3 positives and not so positive outcomes.
- Think about what the PLC learnt about their work as a group and what did the wider school staff learn about the work of the PLC?
- How was this learning mobilised from the PLC to the wider school staff?
- How did the work of the PLC impact on the learning of the students? Could this be measured?
- In what ways would you suggest PLCs work in the future based on your experience?

## Exploring further

The National College publication *Connecting Professional Learning: Leading Effective Collaborative Enquiry across Teaching School Alliances* by Michelle Jones and Alma Harris (2012) is a useful guide outlining the opportunities (and challenges) to facilitating professional learning. The publication can be found at: www.gov.uk/government/uploads/system/uploads/attachment_data/file/335719/Connecting-professional-learning-leading-effective-collaborative-enquiry-across-teaching-school-alliances.pdf

## Useful websites

National CPD Team (2011) *The Learning Rounds Toolkit: Building a Learning Community*: http://issuu.com/nationalcpdteam/docs/the_learning_rounds_tool_kit

*Instructional Rounds for Teaching* [video]: Cindy Luttrell engages in a question and answer session with a teacher (12 minutes) that provides information on how to use a Rounds methodology to engage teachers in improving their own learning. It touches on time, skills and resources needed for this type of activity: www.youtube.com/watch?v=KQ6pLsF9BD0

# Chapter 6
## Clinical practice models

### 6.1 Chapter overview

This chapter will outline:

6.2 introduction and key ideas about clinical practice models; a renewed interest in professional learning based on medically derived models;

6.3 key debates around knowledge mobilisation and implications for education;

6.4 what education can learn from clinical models.

### 6.2 Introduction and key ideas

Renewed interest in modelling teachers' professional learning on clinical practice, a notion first discussed in the 1960s (see Hazard et al, 1967), has triggered more recent proposals from policy makers in the UK, USA and Australia. In particular, the concept of 'Rounds' as a strategy for professional learning in education has been explored. Alter and Coggshall (2009), NCATE (2010), Burn and Mutton (2013) and the Department for Education (DfE, 2015) have proposed a number of possibilities based on medical rounds such as Instructional Rounds (City et al, 2009), Learning Rounds (National CPD Team, 2011), and Teacher Rounds (Del Prete, 2013). More commonly, teachers might recognise these collaborative ventures as professional learning communities (Harris et al, 2018) or Teacher Rounds. These communities have a strong emphasis on collaborative empirical observation and the generation of data through evidence-based approaches apparent in clinical practice and in education (McLean Davies et al, 2013; DfE, 2015a). Combining the Rounds approaches with existing evidence-based teaching might, according to Alter and Coggshall (2009), Conroy et al (2013) and Carter (2015), lead to more effective professional learning for both trainee teachers and those involved in continuing professional development. All these approaches are anchored in evidence-based practice as they adopt a collaborative learning approach that generates and uses a shared evidence-base.

### 6.3 Key debates about knowledge mobilisation and implications for education

There appears to be an unquestioning acceptance that professional learning in medicine is more effective than professional learning in education, and that the medical model is the 'gold standard' to which educationalists must aspire. In the USA, City et al (2009, p 32) claim that *'medicine has... the most powerful practice for analysing and understanding its own work'* and that teaching has *'no such culture building practice'* (p 33) and it is *'an occupation trying to be a profession without a professional practice'* (p 33). Goldacre (2013, p 7) argues along similar lines, stating that *'medicine has leapt forward with evidence-based practice... and asserting that this revolution could – and should – happen in education'*.

While medicine has made great strides in warding off the 'giant evil' of disease (Beveridge, 1942), education has, it appears, gone into reverse, with declining standards and schools that are underperforming (DfE, 2016b). For Goldacre, these matters are related to models of professional learning and many educationalists agree. For them, both professional learning communities and clinical practice models focus on measurable pupil outcomes as an indicator of effective professional learning. There remains, however, the issue that some schools have not been able to demonstrate sufficient improvement based on this metric alone, so regarding the adoption of medical models in teacher education as the silver bullet that will raise standards is problematic. Grimmett et al (2009, p 5) write about *'mimetic isomorphism'* under the influence of *'macro-political neo-liberalist pressures'* in which a group seeks legitimacy by imitating a more successful group who might hold more status. Politically it seems that policy-makers are choosing to use the outcomes of evidence-based practice as a stick to beat the education establishment (or 'the blob' as described by Michael Gove [Gove, 2013]) and to apportion blame to teachers for not only a lack of progress in the development of professional learning strategies but also for raising and falling standards across the education landscape.

In response to these criticisms, the question of the validity of the comparison with medical models of learning has been posed by many academics. Before teachers can adopt the medical model wholesale, there needs to be a greater understanding of the details and realities of medical learning. Rounds approaches, according to Roegman and Riehl (2012, p 926), are based on *'anecdotes, visits and conversations with doctors or mass media portrayals of medical rounds'* rather than research-informed knowledge of the actuality of the learning practices.

There is much evidence to show that the effectiveness of rounds is under-researched (Walton and Steinert, 2010; Prado et al, 2011). There is evidence to suggest that rounds are inefficient in making the best use of learning opportunities (Prado et al, 2011; AlMutar et al, 2013), based on teacher-transmission models (Walton and Steinert, 2010) and made dysfunctional by hierarchies of status (Manias and Street, 2001), and that the beneficiaries of the approach (patients) and the learners (nurses, doctors) are less satisfied than the senior doctors (teachers) (Sweet and Wilson, 2011; AlMutar et al, 2013). While such criticisms of learning in medicine may not apply fully in education, this example shows it is unwise to accept uncritically that the idea of learning in medicine is based on a form of superior practice. If educationalists are to adopt such an approach then they need to understand the limitations as well as the opportunities this approach affords.

When comparing education with medical models, the type of medical practice needs to be taken into account. The Rounds model belongs to biomedicine (which is medicine concerned with medication, surgery or other physical-based treatments) and it is this form of clinical practice often found in teaching hospitals that is envisioned by those advocating the use of such models in education. The discourse adopted by biomedicine such as 'diagnosis' and 'intervention' (OECD, 2011; Kriewaldt and Turnidge, 2013) is now being adopted in education. In the context of educational research, Warren Little (2012) argues for better understanding of teachers' work by using a 'micro-process' approach which methodologically seeks to play close attention to patterns of teacher behaviour and social interactions as they go about their daily work. 'Micro-process' is a systematic method that not only analyses teacher interactions but also reveals how such interactions might impact socially constructed ways of behaving, school structures, processes and the teachers' ideas and personal philosophies of education. This approach is also drawn from a clinical perspective, rooted in the biomedical model and the medical interview between a doctor and patient. In such an interview the objective is to 'silence' the emotions and to limit the patient narrative through the use of a set of short questions and answers. This does not, of course, promote deeper understanding of the patient's medical condition, and medical training has subsequently amended some of its practices as a result of such academic studies.

The purpose of this type of research is to better understand how practitioners create and share meaning through their daily interactions, using methods of observation (videos, for example) to deepen our understanding of their practice (Warren Little, 2012, p 147). These types of 'learning conversations' have proliferated in the USA and New Zealand and have been used to illuminate the ways in which school leaders can understand better how to lead teachers in their interpretation of student data (Earl, 2008).

Other areas of medicine have had to address similar challenges to education with regard to their perceived decline in recent years (Health and Social Care Information Centre, 2016). These challenges are related to the ways in which both mental and public health are linked to wider societal trends such as unemployment, poverty and inequality, to which health professionals are required to respond. Public health, perhaps like education, requires the recipients to accept the intervention as part of their treatment; they need to be actively involved in it in ways that differ from those recipients of biomedicine. The gold standard of biomedicine is that the treatment or intervention works whether or not the recipients believe in it or not, provided they accept the values and practices of the medical professionals. The efficacy of public or mental health interventions will, of course, be inextricably linked to the patient's sense of their own identity, biography and aspirations. In this respect, public health approaches to professional development would appear to be a better fit for education than the biomedical models.

In summary, the argument for evidence-based practice in professional learning that is based on a form of empirical evidence that underpins a profession is not actually axiomatic. The argument is not derived from a robust body of evidence but from 'eminence' – the perceived status and success of medicine, along with 'eloquence' – a rhetorically persuasive argument that is not based on evidence (Lilienfeld et al, 2013).

## 6.4 What can education learn from clinical models?

If we accept that evidence is necessary, but not always sufficient, to raise educational standards, then we need to understand more about the nature of the evidence that will make a difference in education. Looking at the biomedical model of evidence-based practice, Kirmayer (2012) and Lee et al (2013) suggest problematising the fundamental concept of 'evidence'. The commitment in biomedicine is to a positivist ontological and epistemological paradigm which works in this context but does not fully cover public health issues. The reason for this is related to how individuals and communities understand themselves and their experiences – how they culturally define themselves; so the evidence then becomes culturally situated (Kirmayer, 2012; Lee et al, 2013). Whereas biomedical data is more objective and quantifiable, the evidence that speaks for the social world (as opposed to the biological one) is different in its nature. Simply put, one type of evidence-base might be privileged over another, and in terms of 'value for money' the illusion of truth and objectivity imparted by the biomedical model trumps and masks the ideological nature of social explanations and prescriptions and silences alternative explanations, some of which might come from the recipients themselves.

Thinking about culturally situated evidence further complicates this debate, and the notion of transferability between groups of subjects adds to the complexity. Consider, for example, the differences between biomedical interventions based, say, on vaccinations and mental health treatments centred on patient dialogue. Vaccinations are likely to be effective across more than one socio-economic group and their effectiveness can be assessed quite easily. The efficacy of the strategies chosen to assist people with mental health problems is, on the other hand, unlikely to be so clear cut and will depend to a much greater extent on individual patterns of behaviour and personal beliefs/understanding. Questions around the ontology, epistemology and applicability across diverse communities have led to the development of evidence-based practice that is referred to as dialogical bottom-up and top-down models (Green, 2006, 2008; Hunt et al, 2012). These involve practice-based evidence (Green, 2006) as well as evidence-based practice. This practice-based evidence is derived from professionals working with individuals and communities to discover what they need to know and how actions can be taken. In contrast, evidence-based practice is a supposed authoritative prescription that dominates the decision-making process and that can be applied universally without reference to context. This is the model that successive governments have employed although, with the decentralisation of schooling, there are now arguably more opportunities for education professionals to develop practice-based approaches.

In relation to the applicability of evidence across different contexts and the role of practitioners in generating and evaluating evidence in health, the distinction between 'efficacy' and 'effectiveness' (Jacobs et al, 2012; Layde et al, 2012; Lilienfeld et al, 2013) needs to be appreciated. In education these distinctions are not so easily identified. Efficacy research seeks to establish the effects of treatments in tightly controlled standardised conditions. Effectiveness research attempts to establish their effects in real-world situations. The outcomes of the effectiveness research then inform the efficacy research, to provide further evidence for modification of the treatment. Translating this approach from health to education means that practitioner research outcomes would be used to inform centrally agreed or recommended educational policy and to systematically impact on policy outcomes. There is very little evidence that this happens in practice, however, and much practitioner research based on Rounds and professional learning communities focuses on the implementation of policies in schools and does not appear to contribute to the development of wider educational policy (Bottery, 2003; Servage, 2008, 2009).

In health there is growing recognition that an evidence-based approach works best when there are institutional diverse networks (Mercken et al, 2015). Latham et al (2013) suggests it will not be enough to leave teachers or schools to implement a clinical approach to professional learning. There needs to be a supportive architecture for research where researching practitioners have access not only to 'how-to' research or are able to evaluate academic research, but that they also have the time and space in which to do so. Developing such an infrastructure could involve universities, as evidenced through school–university partnerships with Teaching School Alliances, Multi-Academy Trusts and other individual schools.

Teacher trainees on a School Direct programme (school-led, employment-based, postgraduate initial teacher training, leading to Qualified Teacher Status) receive most of their training in school, where they are supported by a mentor, and their academic theory is provided by a local university who works in partnership with the school. Compared with university-based programmes such as the Bachelor of Education (B Ed) or the Postgraduate Certificate of Education (PGCE), where more theory is taught to trainees, academics have noted that while School Direct trainees are generally very good at reflecting on their practice at a technical level, they are less well-schooled in the theory of education, such as the ethical and political aspects of their work. One particular module on their programme challenges trainees to undertake a small piece of research, or teacher inquiry into an aspect of their practice. Academics noted that trainees had most difficulty in understanding a basic methodology for classroom-based research approaches, and had little knowledge about the ethical ramifications of such activities and how to analyse and evaluate the outcomes of their practice. McIntyre (1993) argues that theory can be seen in two forms – as *process* and *content*. For a one-year training programme, with little time spent in the academy, trainees identify more with process knowledge (practical theorising) rather than a wider content base, such as the psychology or history of education. Quoting Alexander (1984, p 146), McIntyre goes on to say that learning to teach is:

> **...a continual process of hypothesis-testing framed by detailed analysis of the values and practical constraints fundamental to teaching. The 'theory' for teacher education should therefore incorporate (i) speculative theory, (ii) the findings of empirical research, (iii) the craft knowledge of practising teachers; but none should be presented as having prescriptive implications for practice; instead students should be encouraged to approach their own practice with the intention of testing hypothetical principles drawn from the consideration of these different types of knowledge.**

## 6.5 Summary

Many policy-makers, academics and some professionals would like teachers to adopt a medical model of learning. Advocates of this model privilege evidence-based practice yet their philosophy for teacher learning appears to be based not on evidence but on eminence or eloquence.

Instead of using medical models 'wholesale' to improve teacher learning, there needs to be more evidence from research into the medical model ways of learning. This would involve understanding both the positive and negative aspects of the model. The evidence in education from Rounds or clinical practice models is currently limited so it would be timely to gain more information from other professions to increase the evidence-base. While acknowledging that claims made here about the different approaches to biomedicine and public health might be rather simplistic and that patients' own medical histories help to form a useful dialogue in deciding on the most appropriate course of action, there is an over-arching belief, especially from policy-makers, that that there is a single 'authoritative' remedy that can be applied to educational practice. An alternative view of evidence-based practice offered by public health models appears to meet the needs of education more closely than those currently favoured by biomedical professionals.

The perception that schools fail to improve is based largely upon policy-makers using the idea of evidence-based practice as a stick to beat the education establishment. Many of the perceived failures of schools (and often in wider society) are directed at schools, and appear elsewhere internationally. Clandinin and Connelly (1996) see this as a 'conduit' down which the 'rhetoric of conclusions' is channelled into schools. Instead of accepting that uncertainty is inevitable in education, governments have perceived these as problematic and the development of evidence-based practice as a way of supplanting these troubling uncertainties with something that is more scientifically based.

There are two perspectives around uncertainty, firstly around the nature of the world (ontological) and secondly about whether we have enough information in the world (epistemological). There is, at present, evidence that epistemological data which is positivistic by nature is privileged over discussions relating to ontological perspectives about different ways of viewing the world. Biesta (2010) notes that these values-based decisions would provide different representations of teacher learning compared with the evidence-based representations that are currently central to the ways we think about improving educational standards. There is no denying that there is much to learn about (and from) medical models. We should not assume, however, that they are superior. We need to have empirical evidence of 'what works' based upon a better understanding of how these models might work in practice before a wholesale adoption is made in education.

- As a teacher, think about how your personal and professional values align with either the ontological or epistemological viewpoint.

- Do you agree with privileging one worldview over the other? Think of reasons for your choice and ways in which this would benefit both students and teachers.

- In relation to your answer to the previous question, what type(s) of evidence should educationalists be sourcing as their knowledge base for teaching?

## Exploring further

The following two publications offer more information about how clinical practice can be used in teacher education:

- Alter, J and Coggshall, J G (2009) Teaching as a Clinical Practice Profession: Implications for Teacher Preparation and State Policy. *National Comprehensive Center for Teacher Quality*: Issue Brief. [online] Available at: https://files.eric.ed.gov/fulltext/ED543819.pdf (accessed 21 April 2018).

- Burn, K and Mutton, T (2013) Review of 'Research-Informed Clinical Practice' in Initial Teacher Education. Research and Teacher Education: The BERA-RSA Inquiry. [online] Available at: www.bera.ac.uk/wp-content/uploads/2014/02/BERA-Paper-4-Research-informed-clinical-practice.pdf (accessed 21 April 2018).

## Useful websites

The origins of clinical teaching in education can be read about in more detail at: www.meshguides.org/guides/node/595

### Note

This chapter is based upon an edited version of Carey Philpott's journal article: Philpott, C (2017) Medical Models for Teachers' Learning: Asking for a Second Opinion. *Journal of Education for Teaching: International Research and Pedagogy*, 43(1): 20–31.

# Chapter 7
# **Planning for implementation**

## 7.1  Chapter overview

This chapter will outline:

7.2   an introduction on how to develop an action plan for evidence-based teaching;

7.3   where you are starting from;

7.4   what you want to achieve;

7.5   the resources there are to help you;

7.6   how you will know when you have achieved it.

## 7.2  Introduction

This chapter outlines an action plan that is intended to help you begin to develop evidence-based teaching in your school. Like all 'prescriptions' for practice in schools, it is important to start by thinking about the particular nature of your context rather than importing a 'one-size-fits-all' solution. Any innovation in practice has to be shaped to fit the particular context you want to use it in.

You also need to be clear about how to evaluate the effects of the innovation rather than assuming that the job is done once the innovation is introduced. It might be that the effects are not what you hoped for, or even what they first appeared to be on the basis of relatively superficial observation. As Karl Marx once wrote, '*all science would be superfluous if outward appearance and the essence of things directly coincided*'. This is a key insight of evidence-based practice: that we need to test everyday impressions with more critically rigorous evaluation, so you need to be clear about what you expect the outcomes to be and how you are going to monitor them.

## 7.3  Where are you starting from?

What are the current strengths and weaknesses of your school in relation to evidence-based teaching?

To what extent are you aware of teaching and learning practices that arise from the following?

- **Pedagogisation** (Watson et al, 2010; Watson, 2014). Watson describes this situation as one in which teachers have been taught to use certain practical strategies as 'research based' but do not necessarily understand the complexity of the underlying research/ideas on which they claim to be based. This means that there is a risk that practices become routinised without sufficient critical scrutiny of whether they are being used appropriately and meaningfully or having any positive effect. Strategies around 'growth mindset' could be a recent example.

- **Acceptance** of government discourse and prescriptions for practice without awareness of the evidence, if any, that underpins it or sufficient evaluation of its effectiveness.

- **Tradition**, 'this is how we do it here'. This can also be related to a type of wider cultural orthodoxy that means that some practices are accepted as normal even though there may be no evidence of whether they are more or less effective than others. Perhaps homework is an example.

- **Fads.** This can be connected to pedagogisation. Some ideas spread from school to school in the form of particular practices without sufficient understanding of either the robustness of the research that underpins them or the nuances and complexity of that research. Brain gym could be a recent example, various approaches to learning styles another.

- **Personal preference.** This can be connected to educational values. I prefer to teach through organising small group discussions rather than whole group teaching. To be honest, I have no evidence about which is more effective.

- **Personal experience.** Personal experience can be an important strand of evidence for evidence-based teaching. However, personal experience can also be subject to limitations. We tend to interpret our experience through our own prior assumptions, which may in themselves be wrong. My personal experience tells me the earth is flat and stationary so the sun and stars must move around the earth. Sometimes personal experience needs insights from research to modify it.

- **Untested assumptions.** These can be related to some of the issues listed previously. Brookfield (1995) identifies three types of assumptions: causal, prescriptive and paradigmatic. Causal assumptions are of the form 'if I do A then it will cause B to happen'. Prescriptive assumptions are about what should be happening, for example 'pupils should be active learners'. Paradigmatic assumptions are the fundamental assumptions that shape the way we understand the world. They are so fundamental that we often think they are just obvious truths about reality rather than assumptions, and we may not even accept that they are assumptions when they are pointed out to us. Perhaps an educational example would be the idea that you need to learn the basics before you can tackle more complicated material.

- **Allowing teachers to teach.** Biesta (2012) argues that teaching has, over recent years, become 'marginalised' and that teaching is now a form of 'control' where the most effective teachers steer children or students to specific learning outcomes to make them, for example, lifelong learners. He sees this as a language of learning or *'learnification'* (Biesta, 2012, p 36). When children or students learn, they learn something and for a purpose and from someone (in this context the teacher). Biesta argues for teachers to be given freedom to teach, to be able to have freedom over subject content, the purpose of education and the building of relationships with their children or students. It could be argued therefore that teachers have been marginalised by prescriptive government agendas and Biesta opines for them to have the courage to teach. Perhaps a good starting point for teachers would be to engage with the latest government White Paper (DfE, 2016a) and to note that while the use of evidence in education is still given priority, the prescriptive agenda still remains, that is, how you, as teacher, should use the evidence. Now might be the time to take courage and reconsider your identity and purpose as a teacher.

## Questions for enquiry in your own school

How and where do you currently use evidence to inform teaching and what type of evidence are you using? Use the questions below to help you to think about this. It is worth remembering that the answers to these questions might be 'patchy'. For example, colleagues undertaking postgraduate qualifications such as Master's degrees might be doing more of this than others. If you have ITE students, they might also be doing more.

- To what extent is there clear evidence of reflective practice such that people are thinking critically about classroom experiences to modify teaching and learning approaches?

- How much practitioner research is taking place?

- What use is currently made of existing sources of research evidence?

- What are those sources and how are they used?

- How much of this use is subject to 'pedagogisation' such that specific practical strategies are adopted without a full understanding of the research that underpins them?

- What knowledge bases are being generated and shared by teachers?

- To what extent is translational research taking place to work out how to apply generic prescriptions to a particular circumstance?

- To what extent is the implementation of practices based on research evidence being rigorously evaluated?

- To what extent is research evidence (from reflection on practice to reports of externally conducted research) being used to develop collective understanding and practice rather than just individual understanding and practice?

- What use is currently made of assessment evidence to inform the development of practice?

- What are the key challenges to developing more evidence-based teaching in your school?

- teachers' attitudes (eg research evidence is irrelevant, unnecessary);

- teachers' confidence in interpreting research and/or conducting practitioner research;

- difficulty accessing appropriate sources of research evidence;

- allocation of sufficient time for teachers to access research or to carry out practitioner research;

- spreading existing pockets of evidence-based teaching more widely.

## 7.4  What do you want to achieve?

The journey to evidence-based teaching might involve several stages, so it is worth thinking about what you want to develop first. Do you want to:

- develop colleagues' awareness of the importance and relevance of research evidence?

- make research evidence more easily accessible to colleagues?

- develop colleagues' confidence and skills in interpreting research evidence?

- develop colleagues' confidence and skills in carrying out practitioner enquiry?

- increase the use of existing data for developing practice?

- generate new data to inform the development of practice?

- spread existing evidence-based teaching more widely?

- increase the extent to which evidence-based teaching practices inform collective development rather than just individual development?

- create more time and space for colleagues to engage in developing evidence-based teaching?

## 7.5  What resources are there to help you?

The most suitable resources to help you will depend on what you want to achieve first.

- If you want to make access to research evidence easier, you might start by looking at some of the websites intended to support evidence-based teaching. However, don't forget the importance of translational research when using these. Some of the most prominent are:

- https://educationendowmentfoundation.org.uk/

- www.meshguides.org/

- www.campbellcollaboration.org/

- http://eppi.ioe.ac.uk/cms/

- If you are particularly interested in randomised controlled trials, a useful resource might be www.nfer.ac.uk/nfer/publications/RCT01/RCT01.pdf.

- If you want to develop the confidence and skills of colleagues in relation to interpreting research and practitioner research, a good resource might be colleagues who are completing or have completed practice-focused higher degrees. They might also be a good resource for developing colleagues' understanding of the value and relevance of educational research.

- Facilitating interaction between colleagues can be done through setting up collaborative practices such as professional learning communities (PLCs) or Rounds approaches (eg Instructional Rounds or Teacher Rounds). These potentially have the dual benefit of focusing on developing practice through gathering evidence and promoting a more collaborative culture of evidence-based development. A number of 'how-to' guides are available.

- If you have ITE students, there are possibilities for using their school-based research projects to promote discussion of evidence-based practice and research in the school. Some schools have successfully organised ITE student-led presentations of their classroom research for groups of staff. Others have set up Rounds approaches (see above) that involve both ITE students and other staff.

- Research in other professional areas suggests that evidence-based practice is most likely to succeed where a number of varied institutions, including universities, collaborate (see for example, Philpott, 2017). So this is an avenue to explore. If your local university education department can see value in researching an aspect of practice jointly with you, it might not require any financial commitment from you to get involved with them.

## 7.6  How will you know when you have achieved it?

As this book is concerned with a wide range of possible approaches to developing evidence-based teaching, it is not possible in this section to identify specific outcomes. These will depend on the approaches you are trying to develop. Instead, this section will focus on some general principles for evaluation with some specific examples.

- Be clear exactly what it is you are trying to achieve so that you will know how to effectively monitor progress.

- Don't mistake increased activity for success. In relation to PLCs and Rounds approaches, for example, teachers can become involved in these without a clear idea of the benefits for practice.

- Be alert to pedagogisation. Are colleagues faithfully implementing the practical steps of a practice but without total clarity about what it is supposed to achieve and whether it is achieving it? For example, how many teachers use peer assessment and self-assessment routinely without a clear view of what it is achieving (if anything)?

- What evidence do you have that the effects of developments in practice are being rigorously monitored and not just evaluated on the basis of superficial impressions? Many teachers say that brain gym approaches make a difference to their pupils. However, there is little, if any, robust evidence.

## 7.7  Summary

It is important to avoid activity becoming an end in itself. One of the best ways to prevent this is to clearly articulate what impact you want the development of evidence-based teaching to have beyond the activity itself. What do you expect to see happening and how will you know when it is happening? Having a clear view of what you expect will enable you to assess more effectively whether it is happening or whether you need to revise or make changes to your approach. Nearly all teaching and learning approaches that claim to be based on evidence are generated elsewhere and need translational research to work out how effective they are and to decide on the best way to implement them in your particular context. So, for these too, you need to be clear what effect they are supposed to be having and how you will know (beyond superficial impressions) that they are having the desired effect.

# Chapter 8
# Conclusions

After 20 years of debate about the use of evidence in education, it appears that we have made little progress in understanding what mode of evidence serves education best, or, indeed, how it should be produced. Likewise, the evaluation of the evidence and its impact on practice, especially with regard to teacher and student learning, remains a challenge for classroom practitioners and school leadership teams.

The 2016 Government White Paper (DfE, 2016a) and the Carter Review of Teacher Training (DfE, 2015) retain a focus on 'research' and 'evidence' but, unlike the 2010 White Paper, omit references to 'teacher inquiry', 'research-informed practice', 'teacher researchers' and similar (Godfrey, 2017). Other 'top-down' messages encourage school leaders to use research to move to a more audit-style culture and to draw upon summaries of research from, for example, the Educational Excellence Everywhere Toolkit:

> **Strong, evidence-informed profession... the effective use of evidence in education... We will continue to work in partnership with the Education Endowment Foundation... expanding its remit to support evidence-based teaching.**

> (DfE, 2016, p 13)

This report goes on to concede that the current evidence-base lacks quality, and is both difficult to translate into practice and challenging for teachers to access. In the Department for Education's (2018) consultation on improving career progression for teachers, the commitment to taking an evidence-based approach and the drive to greater use of research outcomes to understand how best to encourage teacher development is reaffirmed.

However, we still seem to be some way off Slavin's (2002, p 17) vision, which viewed *'education on the brink of a scientific revolution that has the potential to profoundly transform policy, practice and research'.* The relatively new independent Chartered College of Teaching is promoting a research-informed pedagogy with a focus on teachers' stories, so we might at last be acknowledging some link between the perceived 'gold standard' of statistically generated data through randomised controlled trials (RCTs) and systematic literature reviews with other forms of 'truths' held as tacit knowledge by practitioners (Hammersley, 2001; Biesta, 2017). While systematic literature reviews and RCTs might provide a powerful form of evidence-base in education, such evidence should be used in collaboration with other equally significant research models. Adopting a single research method is unlikely to be the best way to address issues in such a complex undertaking as education.

Perhaps as a result of academic, small-scale qualitative studies having little impact on changing teachers' practice, these latest initiatives, with funding from government, along with charitable partners, will begin to provide the necessary infrastructure and support for evidence-based approaches. In an evaluation of *Teaching Schools*, Gu et al (2016) identified a substantial increase in the use of research evidence to inform teaching and learning practices within Teaching School Alliances. In terms of research and development, Gu et al also found that schools were in a stronger position if they partnered with university-based staff able to advise on research approaches and to give general support to teacher research projects (see Churches et al, 2018 and Laroes et al, 2018). In a similar way, teachers who engage with Joint Practice Development (JPD) such as lesson study or research lesson study (Dudley, 2014), Teaching Rounds (Bowe and Gore, 2017; Philpott and Oates, 2017a, b) or as part of a professional learning community (Servage, 2008; Stoll et al, 2018) have greater success in generating useful outcomes for their practice.

Recent government policy linked firmly with the evidence-based/informed agenda is also concerned with interrogating the types of evidence used in the evaluation of the relationship between the cost of provision for professional learning and impact on the value and quality of education. This will be examined as part of an overarching theme addressing two intersecting contexts: the interface of education with economics and the efficacy of existing notions of teacher education and medical education (Baumfield and Mattick, 2017). This may help to provide educators with a form of inter-disciplinary dialogue that we hope will include universities to engender a more systematic change of teacher mindset that begins to close the gap between established research paradigms. In turn, we hope that this leads to a deeper understanding of the value of practitioner investigation as an integral part of academic research. The link with the medical profession might be an opportunity to share 'what works' in practice, but the current mindset (as it appears from government policy) is that education is still a 'problem' waiting to be solved by other, more prestigious professionals rather than teachers themselves.

On a more positive note, it is refreshing to see that the debate about teaching becoming an evidence-informed profession endures. Many of the areas outlined in the chapters of this book still remain contested in education. Changing the hearts and minds of teachers regarding the value of using evidence in their work, whether that be published academic research or their own classroom-based inquiries, remains a challenge for the profession as a whole. There is no 'silver bullet' solution here, and the use and generation of evidence in teaching and learning remains a 'wicked issue'. If we are to support education in its quest to become evidence-based then we need to re-think how we prepare teachers through the multifarious routes to Qualified Teacher Status (QTS) (DfE, 2011) with a career structure that values higher-level study (and rewards teachers accordingly) so that they become *scholars of educational research* (Winch et al, 2015, p 213) and through the inspection regimes.

To help embed the use of locally generated research as central to the health of a school, perhaps is it now time that this should become a reporting strand at Ofsted inspections. Through so doing, schools would be encouraged to focus on the use of data that helps staff evaluate initiatives and to adopt the most appropriate teaching and learning initiatives in their schools.

At a national level and through the Chartered College of Teaching (which would be strengthened by required membership to match other professions), policy decisions should be based on larger-scale studies that serve to inform the profession more widely about national issues that are significant for everyone teaching in the UK.

# References

Alexander, R J (1984) Innovation and Continuity in the Initial Teacher Education Curriculum, in Alexander, R J, Craft, M and Lynch, J (eds) *Change in Teacher Education: Context and Provision since Robbins*. London: Holt, Rinehart and Winston.

AlMutar, S, AlTourah, L, Sadeq, H, Jumanah, K and Marwan, Y (2013) Medical and Surgical Ward Rounds in Teaching Hospitals of Kuwait University: Students' Perception. *Advances in Medical Education and* Practice, 4: 189–93.

Alter, J and Coggshall, J G (2009) Teaching as a Clinical Practice Profession: Implications for Teacher Preparation and State Policy. Issue Brief. New York: *National Comprehensive Center for Teacher Quality.*

Atkinson, E (2000) In Defence of Ideas, or Why "What Works" Is Not Enough. *British Journal of Sociology of Education*, 21(3): 317–30.

Baumfield, V and Mattick, K (2017) *Cost, Value and Quality in Professional Learning: Promoting Economic Literacy in Medical and Teacher Education.* A report from one of the BERA Research Commissions. London: BERA.

Beveridge, W (1942) *Social Insurance and Allied Services*. London: HMSO.

Biesta, G (2017) Education, Measurement and the Professions: Reclaiming a Space for Democratic Professionality in Education. *Educational Philosophy and Theory*, 49(4): 315–30.

Biesta, G (2015) Resisting the Seduction of the Global Education Measurement Industry: Notes on the Social Psychology of PISA. *Ethics and Education*, 10(3): 348–60.

Biesta, G (2012) Giving Teaching Back to Education: Responding to the Disappearance of the Teacher. *Phenomenology & Practice*, 6(2): 35–49.

Biesta, G (2010) Why 'What Works' Still Won't Work: From Evidence-based Education to Value-Based Education. *Studies in Philosophy and Education*, 29(5): 491–503.

Biesta, G (2007) Why "What Works" Won't Work: Evidence-based Practice and the Democratic Deficit in Educational Research, *Educational Theory*, 57(1): 1–22.

Blunkett, D (2000) *Influence or Irrelevance: Can Social Science Improve Government?* Speech to Economic and Social Research Council (ESRC). [online] Available at: www.timeshighereducation.com/news/influence-or-irrelevance/150012.article (accessed 2 February 2018).

Boland, A, Cherry, G and Dickson, R (2014) (eds) *Doing a Systematic Review: A Student's Guide*. London; Thousand Oaks; New Delhi; Singapore: Sage.

Bottery, M (2003) The Leadership of Learning Communities in a Culture of Unhappiness. *School Leadership and Management*, 23(2): 187–207.

Bowe, J and Gore, J (2017) Reassembling Teacher Professional Development: The Case for Quality Teaching Rounds. *Teachers and Teaching: Theory and Practice*, 23(3): 352–66.

British Educational Research Association (BERA) (2014) *Research and the Teaching Profession: Building the Capacity for a Self-improving Education System: Final Report of the BERA-RSA Inquiry into the Role of Research in Teacher Education*. London: BERA. [online] Available at: www.bera.ac.uk/wp-content/uploads/2013/12/BERA-RSA-Research-Teaching-Profession-FULL-REPORT-for-web.pdf?noredirect=1 (accessed 1 February 2018).

*British Educational Research Journal*, 27(5): 575–76.

Brookfield, S (1995) *Becoming a Critically Reflective Teacher*. San Francisco: Jossey-Bass.

Brown, C and Zhang, D (2016) Is Engaging in Evidence-informed Practice in Education Rational? What Accounts for Discrepancies in Teachers' Attitudes Toward Evidence Use and Actual Instances of Evidence Use in Schools? *British Educational Research* Journal, 42(5): 780–801.

Bryman, A (2016) *Social Research Methods* (5th ed). Oxford: Oxford University Press.

Burn, K and Mutton, T (2013) Review of 'Research-Informed Clinical Practice' in Initial Teacher Education. Research and Teacher Education: The BERA-RSA Inquiry. [online] Available at: www.bera.ac.uk/wp-content/uploads/2014/02/BERA-Paper-4-Research-informed-clinical-practice.pdf (accessed 4 February 2018).

Cain, T (2015a) Teachers' Engagement with Published Research: Addressing the Knowledge Problem. *The Curriculum Journal*, 26(3): 488–509.

Cain, T (2015b) Teachers' Engagement with Research Texts: Beyond Instrumental, Conceptual or Strategic Use. *Journal of Education for Teaching*, 41(5): 478–92.

Campbell, C, Pollock, K, Briscoe, P, Carr-Harris, S and Tuters, S (2017) Developing a Knowledge Network for Applied Education Research to Mobilise Evidence in and for Educational Practice. *Education Research*, 59(2): 209–27.

Churches, R, Hall, R and Brookes, J (2018) Closing the Gap: Test and Learn – An Unprecedented National Educational Research Project, in Childs, A and Menter, I (eds) *Mobilising Teacher Researchers: Challenging Educational Inequality*. London; New York: Routledge.

City, E A (2011) Learning from Instructional Rounds. [online] Available at: www.ascd.org/publications/educational-leadership/oct11/vol69/num02/Learning-from-Instructional-Rounds.aspx (accessed 1 February 2018).

City, E A., Elmore, R F, Fiarman, S E and Teitel, L (2009) *Instructional Rounds in Education: A Network Approach to Improving Teaching and Learning.* Cambridge, MA: Harvard Education Press.

Clandinin, D J and Connelly, F M (1996) Teachers' Professional Knowledge Landscapes: Teacher Stories—Stories of Teachers—School Stories—Stories of Schools. *Educational Researcher,* 25(3): 24–30.

Clegg, S (2005) Evidence-based Practice in Educational Research: A Critical Realist Critique of Systematic Review. *British Journal of Sociology of Education,* 26(3): 415–28.

Codd, J (2005) Teachers as 'Managed Professionals' in the Global Education industry: The New Zealand Experience. *Educational Review,* 57(2): 193–206.

Connolly, P (2018) The Future Promise of RCTs in Education: Some Reflections on the Closing the Gap Project, in Childs, A and Menter, I (eds) *Mobilising Teacher Researchers: Challenging Educational Inequality.* London; New York: Routledge.

Conroy, J, Hulme, M and Menter, I (2013) Developing a 'Clinical' Model for Teacher Education. *Journal of Education for Teaching,* 39(5): 557–73.

Cooper, A, Levin, B and Campbell, C (2009) The Growing (But Still Limited) Importance of Evidence in Education Policy and Practice. *Journal of Educational Change,* 10(2–3): 159–71.

Cordingley, P (2008) Research and Evidence-informed Practice: Focusing on Practice and Practitioners. *Cambridge Journal of Education,* 38(1): 37–52.

Davies, P (1999) What is Evidence-based Education? *British Journal of Educational Studies,* 47(2): 108–21.

Day, C (2017) *Teachers' Worlds and Work: Understanding Complexity, Building Quality.* London; New York: Routledge.

Day, C. (1999) *Developing Teachers: The Challenges of Lifelong Learning.* London; Philadelphia: Falmer Press.

Del Prete, T (2013) *Teacher Rounds: A Guide to Collaborative Learning in and for Practice.* Thousand Oaks, CA: Corwin.

Department for Education (DfE) (2018) Strengthening Qualified Teacher Status and Improving Career Progression for Teachers: Government Consultation for

Completion by March 2018. [online] Available at: www.gov.uk/government/consultations/strengthening-qualified-teacher-status-and-career-progression (accessed 1 March 2018).

Department for Education (DfE) (2016a) *Educational Excellence Everywhere: A White Paper Setting Out Our Vision for Schools in England.* London: HMSO. [online] Available at: www.gov.uk/government/uploads/system/uploads/attachment_data/file/508447/Educational_Excellence_Everywhere.pdf (accessed 2 February 2018).

Department for Education (DfE) (2016b) *Intervening in Failing, Underperforming and Coasting Schools: Government Consultation Response.* [online] Available at: www.gov.uk/government/uploads/system/uploads/attachment_data/file/510644/Intervening-in-failing-underperforming-and-coasting-schools-government-response.pdf (accessed 1 February 2018).

Department for Education (DfE) (2015) *Carter Review of Initial Teacher Training (ITT).* Report number: DFE-00036-2015. London: HMSO. [online] Available at: www.gov.uk/government/uploads/system/uploads/attachment_data/file/399957/Carter_Review.pdf (accessed 22 April 2018).

Department for Education (DfE) (2011) *Teachers' Standards: Guidance for School Leaders, School Staff and Governing Bodies.* [online] Available at https://assets.publishing.service.gov.uk/government/uploads/system/uploads/attachment_data/file/665520/Teachers_Standards.pdf (accessed 22 April 2018).

Dewey, J (1929) *The Sources of a Science of Education.* New York: Horace Liveright.

Dimmock, C (2016) Conceptualising the Research-practice-professional Development Nexus: Mobilising School as 'Research-engaged' Professional Learning Communities. *Professional Development in* Education, 42(1): 36–53.

Dray, J, Bowman, J, Freund, M, Campbell, E, Wolfenden, L, Hodder, R and Wiggers, J (2014) Improving Adolescent Mental Health and Resilience through a Resilience-based Intervention in Schools: Study Protocol for a Randomised Controlled Trial. *Trials* 2014, 15: 289. [online] Available at: www.trialsjournal.com/content/15/1/289 (accessed 22 April 2018).

Dudley, P (2014) *Lesson Study: A Handbook.* [online] Available at: http://repositorio.minedu.gob.pe/bitstream/handle/123456789/5017/Lesson%20Study%20a%20Handbook.pdf?sequence=1&isAllowed=y (accessed 5 February 2018).

DuFor, R (2004) What is a 'Professional Learning Community'? *Educational Leadership*, Vol. 61(8) 6–11.

Earl, L (2008) Leadership for Evidence-Informed Conversations, in Earl, L and Timperley, H (eds) *Professional Learning Conversations: Challenges in Using Evidence for Improvement.* New York: Springer.

Educational Endowment Foundation (EEF). [online] Available at: https://educationendowmentfoundation.org.uk (accessed 28 February 2018).

Elliott, J (2001) Making Evidence-Based Practice Educational. *British Educational Research* Journal, 27(5): 555–74.

Ellis, V and McNicholl, J (2015) *Transforming Teacher Education: Reconfiguring the Academic Work*. London; New York: Bloomsbury Academic.

Eraut, M E (1996) Professional Knowledge in Teacher Education, in Nutinen, P (ed) *University of Joensu, Bulletin of the Faculty of Education*, 64: 1–27.

Evans, J and Benefield, P (2001) Systematic Reviews of Educational Research: Does the Medical Model Fit? *British Education Research Journal*, 27(5): 527–41.

Gale, T (2018) What's Not To Like About RCTs in Education? in Childs. A and Menter, I (eds) *Mobilising Teacher Researchers: Challenging Educational Inequality*. London; New York: Routledge.

Godfrey, D (2017) What Is the Proposed Role of Research Evidence in England's 'Self-Improving' School System? *Oxford Review of Education*, 43(4): 433–46.

Goldacre, B (2013) *Building Evidence into Education*. [online] Available at: www.gov.uk/government/news/building-evidence-into-education (accessed 13 September 2017).

Goodwin, A L, Del Prete, T, Reagan, E M and Roegman, R (2015) A Closer Look at the Practice and Impact of "Rounds". *International Journal of Educational Research*, 73: 37–43.

Goodwin, M, Greasley, S, Richardson, P J and Richardson, L (2010) Can We Make Environmental Citizens? A Randomised Control Trial of the Effects of a School-Based Intervention on the Attitudes and Knowledge of Young People. *Environmental* Politics, 19(3): 392–412.

Gorard, S and Torgerson, C (2006) *The ESRC Researcher Development Initiative: Promise and Pitfalls of Pragmatic Trials in Education*. Paper presented at the British Educational Research Association Annual Conference, University of Warwick, 6–9 September 2006.

Gove, M (2013) I Refuse to Surrender to the Marxist Teachers Hell-Bent on Destroying Our Schools: Education Secretary Berates 'the New Enemies of Promise' for Opposing His Plans. *Daily Mail*, March 23. [online] Available at: www.dailymail.co.uk/debate/article-2298146/ (accessed 1 February 2018).

Green, L W (2008) Making Research Relevant: If It is an Evidence-Based Practice, Where's the Practice-Based Evidence? Family Practice, 25: Suppl 1: i20–24. [online] Available at: www.ncbi.nlm.nih.gov/pubmed/18794201 (accessed 25 April 2018).

Green, L W (2006) Public Health Asks of Systems Science: To Advance Our Evidence-Based Practice, Can You Help Us Get More Practice-Based Evidence? *American Journal of Public Health.* [online] Available at http://ajph.aphapublications.org/doi/pdf/10.2105/AJPH.2005.066035 (accessed 24 April 2018).

Grimmett, P, Fleming, R and Trotter, L (2009) Legitimacy and Identity in Teacher Education: A Micro-Political Struggle Constrained by Macro-Political Pressures. *Asia-Pacific Journal of Teacher* Education, 37(1): 5–26.

Gu, Q, Rea, S, Smethem, L, Dunford, J, Varley, M, Sammons, P, Parish, N, Armstrong, P and Powell, L (2016) *Teaching Schools Evaluation.* National College for Teaching and Leadership: Final Report. London: DfE.

Hall, E (2009) Engaging in and Engaging with Research: Teacher Inquiry and Development. *Teachers and Teaching*, 15(6): 669–81.

Hammersley, M (2005) Is the Evidence-Based Practice Movement Doing More Good Than Harm? Reflections on Iain Chalmers' Case for Research-Based Policy Making and Practice. *Evidence and Policy,* 1(1): 85–100.

Hammersley, M (2001) On 'Systematic' Reviews of Research Literatures: A 'Narrative' Response to Evans and Benefield. *British Educational Research Journal*, 27(5): 544–54.

Hammersley, M (1997) Educational Research and Teaching: A Response to David Hargreaves' TTA Lecture. *British Educational Research Journal*, 23(2): 141–61.

Hammersley-Fletcher, L, Lewin, C, with Davies, C, Duggan, J, Rowley, H and Spink, E (2015) Evidence-Based Teaching: Advancing Capability and Capacity for Enquiry in Schools. Interim Report. National College for Teaching and Leadership. London: DfE. [online] Available at: www.gov.uk/government/publications/evidence-based-teaching-advancing-capability-and-capacity-for-enquiry-in-schools-interim-report (accessed 25 April 2018).

Hargreaves, A and Fullan, M (2012) *Professional Capital: Transforming Teaching in Every School.* New York: Teachers College Press.

Hargreaves, D (1999) The Knowledge-Creating School. *British Journal of Educational Studies,* 47(2): 122–44.

Hargreaves, D (1998) A New Partnership of Stakeholders and a National Strategy for Research in Education, in Rudduck, J and McIntyre, D (eds) *Challenges for Educational Research.* London: Paul Chapman.

Hargreaves, D (1996) Teaching as Research Based Profession: Possibilities and Prospects. *The Teacher Training Agency Annual Lecture.* [online] Available at:

https://eppi.ioe.ac.uk/cms/Portals/0/PDF%20reviews%20and%20summaries/TTA%20Hargreaves%20lecture.pdf (accessed 2 February 2018).

Harris, A, Jones, M and Huffman, J (2018) (eds) *Teachers Leading Educational Reform: The Power of Professional Learning Communities*. London; New York: Routledge.

Hazard, W, Chandler, B and Stiles, L. (1967) The Tutorial and Clinical Program for Teacher Education. *Journal of Teacher* Education, 18(3): 269–76.

Health and Social Care Information Centre (2016) [online] Available at: www.hscic.gov.uk (accessed 25 April 2018).

Hemsley-Brown, J and Sharp, C (2003) The Use of Research to Improve Professional Practice: A Systematic Review of the Literature. *Oxford Review of Education*, 29(4): 449–70.

Hillage, J, Pearson, R, Anderson, A and Tamkin, P (1998) *Excellence in Research on Schools*. London: DfEE. [online] Available at: http://dera.ioe.ac.uk/9856/1/RR74.pdf (accessed 25 April 2018).

Holmlund Nelson, T, Deuel, A, Slavit, D and Kennedy, A (2010) Leading Deep Conversations in Collaborative Inquiry Groups. *The Clearing House: A Journal of Educational Strategies, Issues and* Ideas, 83(5): 175–79.

Hoyle, E (1974) Professionality, Professionalism and Control in Teaching. *London Education Review,* 3(2): 13–19.

Hunt, J, Curran, G, Kramer, T, Mouden, S, Ward-Jones, S, Owen, R and Fortney, J. (2012) Partnership for Implementation of Evidence-Based Mental Health Practices in Rural Federally Qualified Health Centers: Theory and Methods. *Progress in Community Health Partnerships: Research, Education and* Action, 6(3): 389–98.

Hutchison, D and Styles, B (2010) *A Guide to Running Randomised Controlled Trials for Educational Researchers*. Slough: NFER. [online] Available at: www.nfer.ac.uk/publications/RCT01/ (accessed 25 April 2018).

Jacobs, J, Jones, E, Gabella, B, Spring, B and Brownson, R (2012) Tools for Implementing an Evidence-Based Approach in Public Health Practice. *Preventing Chronic* Disease, 9: 110324. doi: 10.5888/pcd9.110324.

Jones, K (2017) Collaboration, Creativity and Capital in Professional Learning Contexts. *Professional Development in* Education, 43(1): 1–5.

Jones, S-L, Procter, R and Younie, S (2015) Participatory Knowledge Mobilisation: An Emerging Model for International Translational Research in Education. *Journal of Education for Teaching: International Research and Pedagogy*, 41(5): 555–73.

Joyce, B (2004) How Are Professional Learning Communities Created? History Has a Few Messages. *Phi Delta Kappan*, 86(1): 76–83.

Kirmayer, L (2012) Cultural Competence and Evidence-Based Practice in Mental Health: Epistemic Communities and the Politics of Pluralism. *Social Science and* Medicine, 75(2): 249–56.

Kriewaldt, J and Turnidge, D (2013) Conceptualising an Approach to Clinical Reasoning in the Education Profession. *Australian Journal of Teacher* Education, 38(6): 103–15.

Laroes, E, Bronkhorst, L H, Akkerman, S F and Wubbels, T (2018) Teacher-Researchers' Expanding Perceptions of Research in a School-University Collaborative Research Project, in Childs, A and Menter, I (eds) *Mobilising Teacher Researchers: Challenging Educational Inequality.* London; New York: Routledge.

Latham, J, Murajda, L, Forland, F and Jansen, A (2013) Capacities, Practices and Perceptions of Evidence-Based Public Health in Europe. *Eurosurveillance*, 18(10. [online] Available at: www. eurosurveillance.org/ViewArticle. aspx?ArticleId=20421 (accessed 1 February 2018).

Lave, J (1991) *Situated Learning: Legitimate Peripheral Participation.* Cambridge: Cambridge University Press.

la Velle, L (2015) Translational Research and Knowledge Mobilisation in Teacher Education: Towards a 'Clinical', Evidence-Based Profession? *Journal of Education for Teaching: International Research and Pedagogy*, 41(5): 460–63.

Layde, P, Christiansen, A, Peterson, D, Guse, C, Maurana, C and Brandenburg, T (2012) A Model to Translate Evidence-Based Interventions into Community Practice. *American Journal of Public Health*, 102(4): 617–24.

Leask, M (2011) Improving the Professional Knowledge Base for Education: Using Knowledge Management and Web 2.0 Tools. *Policy Futures in Education*, 9(5): 644–60.

Lee, H, Fitzpatrick, J and Baik, S (2013) Why Isn't Evidence Based Practice Improving Health Care for Minorities in the United States? *Applied Nursing* Research, 26(4): 263–68.

Levin, B (2008) *How to Change 500 Schools: A Practical and Positive Approach for Leading Change at Every Level.* Cambridge, MA: Harvard Education Press.

Lilienfeld, S, Ritschel, L, Lynn, S, Cautin, R and Latzman, R (2013) Why Many Clinical Psychologists Are Resistant to Evidence-Based Practice: Root Causes and Constructive Remedies. *Clinical Psychology* Review, 33(7): 883–900.

MacLure, M (2005) 'Clarity Bordering on Stupidity': Where's the Quality in Systematic Review? *Journal of Education Policy*, 20(4): 393–416.

Manias, E and Street, A (2001) Nurse–Doctor Interactions during Critical Care Ward Rounds. *Journal of Clinical Nursing*, 10(4): 442–50.

McIntyre, D (1993) Theory, Theorizing and Reflection in Initial Teacher Education, in Calderhead, J and Gates, P (eds) *Conceptualizing Reflection in Teacher Development.* London; Washington, DC: The Falmer Press.

Mercken, L, Saul, J, Lemaire, R, Valente, T and Leischow, S (2015) Coevolution of Information Sharing and Implementation of Evidence-Based Practices Among North American Tobacco Cessation Quitlines. *American Journal of Public Health,* 105(9): 1814–22.

National Council for Accreditation of Teacher Education (NCATE) (2010) *Transforming Teacher Education Through clinical practice: A National Strategy to Prepare Effective Teachers.* Report of the Blue Ribbon panel on clinical preparation and partnerships for improved student learning. Washington, D.C.: NCATE. [online] Available at: www.highered.nysed.gov/pdf/NCATECR.pdf (accessed 10 March 2018).

NationalCPD Team (2011) The Learning Rounds Toolkit. [online] Available at: https://issuu.com/nationalcpdteam/docs/the_learning_rounds_tool_kit_ updated_(accessed 30 April 2018).

National Education Union (2018) Global Education 'Reform' Movement. [online] Available at: www.teachers.org.uk/edufacts/germ (accessed 1 February 2018).

Nelson, J and O'Beirne, C (2014) *Using Evidence in the Classroom: What Works and Why?* Slough: NFER. [online] Available at: www.nfer.ac.uk/publications/IMPA01 (accessed 1 February 2018).

Oakley, A (2003) Research Evidence, Knowledge Management and Educational Practice: Early Lesson from a Systematic Approach. *London Review of Education*, 1(1): 21–33.

Oakley, A (2002) Social Science and Evidence-Based Everything. *Educational Review*, 54(3): 277–86.

Oakley, A (2001) Making Evidence-Based Practice Education: A Rejoinder to John Elliott.

Oakley, A, Gough, D, Oliver, S and Thomas, J (2005) The Politics of Evidence and Methodology: Lessons from the EPPI-Centre. *Evidence and Policy: A Journal of Research, Debate and Practice*, 1(1): 5–32.

Oates, T (2007) Protecting the Innocent – The Need for Ethical Frameworks within Mass Educational Innovation, in Saunders, L (ed) *Educational Research and Policy-Making – Exploring the Border Country Between Research and Policy.* Abingdon: Routledge.

OECD (2016) School Leadership for Development of Professional Learning Communities. *Teaching in Focus,* 2016/15 (September): 1-4. [online] Available at www.oecd-ilibrary.org/education/school-leadership-for-developing-professional-learning-communities_5jlr5798b937-en (accessed 25 April 2018).

OECD (2011) *Building a High Quality Teaching Profession: Lessons from around the World.* [online] Available at: www.oecd.org/edu/school/programmefor internationalstudentassessmentpisa/ (accessed 1 February 2018).

Ovenden-Hope, T and la Velle, L (2015) Translational Research in Education for Knowledge Mobilisation: A Study of Use and Teacher Perception in Primary Schools in England, UK. *Journal of Education for Teaching: International Research and Pedagogy,* 41(5): 574–85.

Pedder, D and Opfer, D (2011) Are We Realising the Full Potential of Teachers' Professional Learning in Schools in England? Policy Issues and Recommendations from a National Study. *Professional Development in Education,* 37(5): 741–58.

Philpott, C (2017) Medical Models for Teachers' Learning: Asking for a Second Opinion. *Journal of Education for Teaching: International Research and Pedagogy,* 43(1): 20–31.

Philpott, C and Oates, C (2017a) Teacher Agency and Professional Learning Communities: What Can Learning Rounds in Scotland Teach Us? *Professional Development in* Education, 43(3): 318–33.

Philpott, C and Oates, C (2017b) Professional Learning Communities and Drivers of Educational Change: The Case of Learning Rounds. *Journal of Educational Change,* 18: 209–34. doi:10.1007/s10833-016-9278-4

Philpott, C and Oates, C (2015) What Do Teachers Do When They Say They Are Doing Learning Rounds? Scotland's Experience of Instructional Rounds. *European Journal of Educational Research,* 4(1): 22–37.

Poultney, H (2017) Case Study 2: Active Learning, in Poultney, V. (ed) *Evidence-Based Teaching in Primary Education.* St Albans: Critical Publishing.

Poultney, V (2017) What Have We Learnt from Engaging with Evidence-Based Teaching? in Poultney, V (ed) *Evidence-Based Teaching in Primary Education.* St Albans: Critical Publishing.

Prado, H, Falbo, G, Falbo, A and Figueiroa, J (2011) Active Learning on the Ward: Outcomes from a Comparative Trial with Traditional Methods. *Medical Education*, 45(3): 273–79.

Prenger, R, Poortman, C and Handelzalts, A (2017) Factors Influencing Teachers' Professional Development in Networked Professional Learning Communities. *Teaching and Teacher Education*, 68: 77–90.

Reece, A and Klaber, R (2012) Maximising Learning on Ward Rounds. *Archives of Disease in Childhood Education and Practice Education*, 97(2): 61–67. [online] Available at: http://ep.bmj.com/content/97/2/61 (accessed 25 April 2018).

Rickinson, M, Sebba, J and Edwards, A (2011) *Improving Research through User Engagement*. London; New York: Routledge.

Roberts, J (2012) *Instructional Rounds in Action*. Cambridge, MA: Harvard Education Press.

Roegman, R and Riehl, C (2015) Playing Doctor with Teacher Preparation: An Examination of Rounds as a Socializing Practice for Preservice Teachers. *International Journal of Educational Research*, 73: 89–99.

Roegman, R and Riehl, C (2012) Playing Doctor with Education: Considerations in Using Medical Rounds as a Model for Instructional Rounds. *Journal of School Leadership*, 22: 922–52.

Ryan, W and Gilbert, I (eds) (2011) *Inspirational Teachers, Inspirational Learners: A Book of Hope for Creativity and the Curriculum in the Twenty First Century*. Camarthen: Crown House Publishing.

Sahlberg, P (2012) How is GERM Infecting Schools Around the World? [online] Available at: https://pasisahlberg.com/text-test/ (accessed 25 April 2018).

Servage, L (2009) Who is the "Professional" in a Professional Learning Community? An Exploration of Teacher Professionalism in Collaborative Professional Development Settings. *Canadian Journal of Education*, 32(1): 149–71.

Servage, L (2008) Critical and Transformative Practices in Professional Learning Communities. *Teacher Education* Quarterly, 35(1): 63–76.

Schön, D (1983) *The Reflective Practitioner: How Professionals Think in Action*. New York: Basic Books.

Segedin, S (2017) Theatre as a Vehicle for Mobilising Knowledge in Education. *International Journal of Education and the Arts*, 18(15): 2–13.

Shavelson, R, Phillips, D and Towne, L (2003) On the Science of Education Design Studies. *Educational Researcher*, 32(1): 25–28.

Shulman, L S (1987) Knowledge and Teaching: Foundations of the New Reform. *Harvard Educational Review*, 57(1): 1–22.

Slavin, R (2002) Evidence-Based Education Policies: Transforming Educational Practice and Research. *Educational Researcher*, 31(7): 15–21.

Smith, F and Hardman, F (2000) Evaluating the Effectiveness of the National Literacy Strategy: Identifying Indicators of Success. *Educational* Studies, 26(3): 365–78.

Stenhouse, L (1975) *An Introduction to Curriculum Research and Development.* London: Heinemann.

Stoll, L, Bolam, R, McMahon, A, Wallace, M and Thomas, S (2006) Professional Learning Communities: A Review of the Literature. *Journal of Educational* Change, 7(4): 221–58.

Stoll, L, Brown, C, Spence-Thomas, K and Taylor, C (2018) Teacher Leadership Within and Across Professional Learning Communities, in Harris, A, Jones, M and Huffman, J B (eds) *Teachers Leading Educational Reform: The Power of Professional Learning Communities.* Oxon; New York: Routledge.

Sweet, G and Wilson, H (2011) A Patient's Experience of Ward Rounds. *Patient Education and* Counseling, 84(2): 150–51.

Teitel, L (2009) Improving Teaching and Learning through Instructional Rounds. *Harvard Education Letter*, 25(3): 1–3.

Tooley, J and Darby, D (1998) *Educational Research: A Critique: A Survey of Published Educational Research. Report presented to OFSTED.* [online] Available at: www.voced.edu.au/content/ngv%3A15631 (accessed 2 February 2018).

Torgerson, C (2009) Randomised Controlled Trials in Education Research: A Case Study of an Individually Randomised Pragmatic Trial. *Education 3-13*, 37(4): 313–21.

Torgerson, C (2001) The Need for Randomised Controlled Trials in Educational Research. *British Journal of Educational Studies*, 49(3): 316–28.

Torgerson, C, Torgerson, D, Birks, Y and Porthouse, J (2005) A Comparison of Randomised Controlled Trials in Health and Education. *British Educational Research Journal*, 31(6): 761–85.

Torgerson, D and Torgerson, C (2003) Avoiding Bias in Randomised Controlled Trials in Educational Research. *British Journal of Educational Studies*, 51(1): 36–45.

Trowsdale, J and Richardson, A (2017) Colour-Coding for Development of Writing in Year 3, Poultney, V (ed) *Evidenced-Based Teaching in Primary Education.* St Albans: Critical Publishing.

Voelkel Jr, R and Chrispeels, J (2017) Understanding the Link Between Professional Learning Communities and Teacher Collective Efficacy. *School Effectiveness and School Improvement*, 28(4): 505–26.

Walton, J and Steinert, Y (2010) Patterns of Interaction During Rounds: Implications for Work-Based Learning. *Medical* Education, 44(6): 550–58.

Warren Little, J (2012) Understanding Data Use Practice Among Teachers: The Contribution of Micro-Process Studies. *American Journal of Education*, 118(2): 143–66.

Watson, A, Kehler, M and Martino, W (2010) The Problem of Boys' Literacy Underachievement: Raising Some Questions. *Journal of Adolescent & Adult Literacy* 53(5): 356–61.

Watson, C (2014) Effective Professional Learning Communities? The Possibilities for Teachers as Agents of Change in Schools. *British Educational Research Journal*, 40(1): 18–29.

Wiliam, D (2014) Why Teaching Will Never Be a Research-Based Profession and Why That's a Good Thing. *ResearchED National Conference*. Raine's Foundation School, London.

Willegems, V, Consuegra, E, Struyven, K and Engels, N (2017) Teachers and Pre-Service Teachers as Partners in Collaborative Teacher Research: A Systematic Literature Review. *Teaching and Teacher Education*, 64: 230–45.

Winch, C, Oancea, A and Orchard, J (2015) The Contribution of Educational Research to Teachers' Professional Learning: Philosophical Understandings. *Oxford Review of Education*, 41(2): 202–16.

# Index